The rapid growth of academic literature in the field of economics has posed serious problems for both students and teachers of the subject. The latter find it difficult to keep pace with more than a few areas of their subject, so that an inevitable trend towards specialism emerges. The student quickly loses perspective as the maze of theories and models grows and the discipline accommodates an increasing amount of quantitative techniques.

'Macmillan Studies in Economics' is a new series which sets out to provide the student with short, reasonably critical surveys of the developments within the various specialist areas of theoretical and applied economics. At the same time, the studies aim to form an integrated series so that, seen as a whole, they supply a balanced overview of the subject of economics. The emphasis in each study is upon recent work, but each topic will generally be placed in a historical context so that the reader may see the logical development of thought through time. Selected bibliographies are provided to guide readers to more extensive works. Each study aims at a brief treatment of the salient problems in order to avoid clouding the issues in detailed argument. Nonetheless, the texts are largely self-contained, and presume only that the student has some knowledge of elementary micro-economics and macro-economics.

Mathematical exposition has been adopted only where necessary. Some recent developments in economics are not readily comprehensible without some mathematics and statistics, and quantitative approaches also serve to shorten what would otherwise be lengthy and involved arguments. Where authors have found it necessary to introduce mathematical techniques, these techniques have been kept to a minimum. The emphasis is upon the economics, and not upon the quantitative methods. Later studies in the series will provide analyses of the links between quantitative methods, in particular econometrics, and economic analysis.

MACMILLAN STUDIES IN ECONOMICS

General Editors: D. C. ROWAN and G. R. FISHER

Executive Editor: D. W. PEARCE

Published

John Burton: WAGE INFLATION
Miles Fleming: MONETARY THEORY
C. J. Hawkins and D. W. Pearce: CAPITAL INVESTMENT APPRAISAL
David F. Heathfield: PRODUCTION FUNCTIONS
D. W. Pearce: COST-BENEFIT ANALYSIS
David Robertson: INTERNATIONAL TRADE POLICY
R. Shone: THE PURE THEORY OF INTERNATIONAL TRADE
Frank J. B. Stilwell: REGIONAL ECONOMIC POLICY
Grahame Walshe: INTERNATIONAL MONETARY REFORM

Forthcoming

E. R. Chang: PRINCIPLES OF ECONOMIC ACCOUNTING
G. Denton: ECONOMICS OF INDICATIVE PLANNING
N. Gibson: MONETARY POLICY
C. J. Hawkins: THEORY OF THE FIRM
D. Jackson: ACCOUNTING FOR POVERTY
P. N. Junankar: INVESTMENT FUNCTIONS
J. E. King: LABOUR ECONOMICS
J. Kregel: THEORY OF ECONOMIC GROWTH
D. Mayston: THE POSSIBILITY OF SOCIAL CHOICE
G. McKenzie: MONETARY THEORY OF INTERNATIONAL TRADE
S. K. Naith: WELFARE ECONOMICS
A. Peaker: BRITISH ECONOMIC GROWTH SINCE 1945
F. Pennance: HOUSING ECONOMICS
Maurice Peston: PUBLIC GOODS AND THE PUBLIC SECTOR
C. Rowley: ANTI-TRUST ECONOMICS
C. Sharp: TRANSPORT ECONOMICS
G. K. Shaw: FISCAL POLICY
P. Simmons: DEMAND THEORY
M. Stabler: AGRICULTURAL ECONOMICS
M. Townsend: MONETARISM VERSUS KEYNESIANISM
M. Townsend: QUANTITY THEORY OF MONEY
John Vaizey: ECONOMICS OF EDUCATION
P. Victor: ECONOMICS OF POLLUTION
J. Wiseman: PRICING PROBLEMS OF THE NATIONALISED INDUSTRIES

International Trade Policy

DAVID ROBERTSON

Lecturer in Economics, University of Reading

Macmillan

First published 1972 by
THE MACMILLAN PRESS LTD
London and Basingstoke
Associated companies in New York Toronto
Dublin Melbourne Johannesburg and Madras

SBN 333 13371 4

Printed in Great Britain by
THE ANCHOR PRESS LTD
Tiptree, Essex

Contents

Acknowledgements

An earlier draft of this pamphlet was read by a number of persons whose valuable comments have helped to remove inaccuracies and obscurities from the text. In particular I should like to express my thanks for comments from Professor Ivor Pearce and Dr George McKenzie, of the University of Southampton, Mr Ronald Shone of the University of Sheffield, and to Mr B. J. P. Fall of the Civil Service College, London Centre. Any omissions, inaccuracies or obscurities that remain are entirely the responsibility of the author.

D. R.

1 Introduction

International trade flows are influenced, directly and indirectly, by a wide variety of economic policy measures. It is essential, therefore, to begin with a definition of trade policy. Professor Meade [41] chose to restrict the subject to 'those policies which aim directly at controlling particular elements in the balance of payments', which already neglects the indirect effects on international transactions of domestic tax and subsidy policies on non-traded goods and services. In this survey it is proposed to restrict the discussion even further and to concentrate on measures for regulating merchandise trade flows. The diversity of service transactions composing the 'invisible' accounts of the balance of payments prohibits a comprehensive examination, but in any case it would involve surveying a largely uncharted area.[1]

Trade policy is principally concerned with resource allocation. An import duty or an export subsidy on a particular commodity protects the domestic producers and the productive resources they employ; both devices encourage resources to shift into, or remain in, the protected activity. Protection is not the only motive, however, for implementing trade policy measures. They may, for example, be introduced for balance of payments reasons, or to alter consumption patterns in a desired manner, or to exploit foreign suppliers or markets; historically, taxes on trade have been important sources of government revenue too, although this is now generally a minor consideration. Whatever the motive, however, the effect of trade policy is to reallocate economic resources. The

[1] Measures used to regulate income and expenditure on invisibles appear to be mainly financial (e.g. exchange controls), but in many instances it is difficult to assess the effectiveness of such measures.

main interest, therefore, is in the protective effects of trade policy on overall welfare and income distribution.

The aim of this survey is to show how the theory of trade policy has advanced in recent years, stimulated by new issues that have arisen as a result of changes in the international economy. Traditionally, trade policy has concentrated on tariffs, but most of the conclusions have been readily adapted to other trade interventions. The evolution of the theory of second best has prompted a reassessment of the arguments for tariffs which has caused revisions in the traditional approach to the welfare effects of trade policy. In addition, the efficiency of trade policy structures has received much attention with the realisation that the positive aspects of trade policy are an important component in any choice between alternative policies affecting resource allocations.

Three specific issues in trade policy have been singled out for special treatment in this survey. As international agreements have reduced tariffs and almost completely eliminated quantitative restrictions on trade in manufactured goods (at least on trade between advanced industrial countries), other types of trade restraint have become relatively more significant. These non-tariff distortions are very varied and complex and cannot be treated within a single theory, but the problems they create and the special problems of agricultural trade are discussed below. A second subject of special interest concerns the theory of customs unions, which is an aspect of the theory of second best. The rapid increase in discriminatory regional trade agreements is undermining the framework of multilateralism that has been the basis of international commercial policy since 1945, and deeper understanding of its effects is necessary. Finally, separate consideration is given to the pressing problems of trade policy for less developed countries.

In order to simplify the discussion of trade policy, it is assumed throughout this survey that countries are operating with fixed exchange rates which apply to all imports and exports. Multiple exchange rates and differential exchange control regulations, which are direct substitutes for most trade policy measures, are then excluded. Since most countries – all developed countries – operate fixed exchange rates according

12

to IMF regulations, this is a realistic assumption. Because of the convention of fixed exchange rates, with only very infrequent adjustments, trade policy measures represent devices for discriminating the rates at which products are exchanged in international trade; for example, a tariff structure establishes, in effect, a set of multiple import rates, which discriminate against exports also (see Bhagwati [9]).

A NOTE ON INTERNATIONAL INSTITUTIONS

When the International Monetary Fund (IMF) and the International Bank for Reconstruction and Development (World Bank) were established in 1944 at the Bretton Woods Conference, it was intended that a sister organisation to supervise international trade policies should be constituted later. Conflicts of interest between the United States Administration as the main proponent of free trade and the European countries' concern for national priorities of full employment and reconstruction protracted the negotiations for the International Trade Organisation (ITO). Eventually the ITO Charter was drafted in 1949 but it was never ratified by governments. Instead the General Agreement on Tariffs and Trade (GATT), which was a temporary expedient devised in 1947 in anticipation of ITO, has developed into the major organisation dealing with trade policy matters (see Curzon [17], Patterson [50]).

GATT, despite its uncertain origins, has made a substantial contribution to the development of the world economy by introducing some measure of order into international trading relations after the anarchy of the 1930s, and by supervising the liberalisation of tariffs. Nevertheless, this 'temporary' organisation has little power to control its 'Contracting Parties'. Initial reservations about inadequacies in the basic principles of the General Agreement were overcome by adaptations and revision. But they have given way to more fundamental doubts about the uniformity with which its rules have been applied: some countries have doubts because they consider the rules are not uniformly applied but are moulded

13

to meet special situations (e.g. the United States view of certain measures adopted by the EEC); while others consider that the uniformity with which the rules are applied is unfair (e.g. the less developed countries' demands for non-reciprocity and the right to preferences, which have been partly taken into account in Part IV of the General Agreement).

In the first decade after 1945, tariffs were not the most important restraint on international trade. Quota restrictions and exchange controls operated by the countries of Western Europe were the main barriers. The Organisation for European Economic Co-operation (OEEC), established in 1948 to administer Marshall Aid and to co-ordinate economic recovery, gradually during the 1950s eliminated almost all quotas on intra-West European trade in industrial products and introduced multilateralism into international payments. In 1961, when the tasks of the OEEC were almost completed, the United States and Canada gave up their associate status and became full members of a new organisation, the Organisation for Economic Co-operation and Development (OECD). Subsequently Japan also joined OECD, which makes that organisation the centre for economic co-operation among the advanced industrial countries.

One of the stated aims of OEEC was to establish a single integrated market in Western Europe. Throughout the 1950s much effort was expended towards this end in OEEC and in other organisations. Details of the many initiatives and the conflicts they created can be found in Camps [10], PEP [53] and a number of other sources. In January 1958, the European Economic Community (EEC) was established according to the Treaty of Rome.[1] A belated attempt by Britain to establish a free trade area comprising all the OEEC members, intended to neutralise the expected effects on trade of the Treaty of Rome, failed in 1959. Subsequently, the European Free Trade Association (EFTA) was established by the Stockholm Convention in 1960 (see Corbet and Robertson [14]). This division of

[1] In mid-1967 the European Economic Community, the European Coal and Steel Community and Euratom merged and became known as the European Communities. The familiar abbreviation, EEC, will be used throughout this survey.

the major West European countries has persisted ever since, despite many attempts to reconcile the two trading blocs.

During the 1960s, trade policy became more relevant for less developed countries. United Nations regional economic commissions had been concerned with development policies for some time, but as the number of colonial territories achieving independence grew, the demands for economic development assistance and trading opportunities in developed countries increased. In addition, regional trading groups were formed in Latin America and Africa (see Kahnert *et al.* [34]). The growing urgency of the less developed countries' demands for development assistance, and their general dissatisfaction with GATT as a forum in which pressure could be exerted on advanced industrial countries, led to the 1964 United Nations Conference on Trade and Development (UNCTAD). At the conference the less developed countries united into a more-or-less common front. One consequence was that UNCTAD was established as a permanent U.N. agency, which now provides the less developed countries with a forum in which they are able to unite to confront the developed countries of the world with their development needs.

2 Theory of Tariffs

Most theoretical analysis of trade policy is undertaken in terms of tariffs – that is, duties levied on imports. There are a number of good reasons for this. First, tariffs are the single device employed most widely for regulating trade flows. Second, except under special circumstances, tariffs are the only measure of trade regulation permitted by GATT. Third, they operate through the price mechanism which represents the heart of modern economic theory. In consequence, tariff analysis can be readily adapted to encompass other trade controls which operate through the price mechanism; for example, export duties and subsidies, import subsidies and quotas and several other types of non-tariff barrier.

THE CASE FOR FREE TRADE

In order to analyse arguments for tariffs and other trade restrictions it is first necessary to understand the conditions for optimum welfare under free trade. Samuelson [55] has shown that free trade is superior to a situation with no trade. He has also established that some trade is superior to no trade; but this does not mean that any trade is better than no trade because any trade (excluding free trade) is a suboptimal state, as is no trade. Hence, both are second-best situations which cannot be ranked. (The theory of second best is discussed below; for a concise summary of the gains from trade theorem, see Shone [57].)

The standard model of international trade simplifies the problem to only two commodities (X and Y), and two factors of production available in fixed quantities. Both commodities have production functions which are subject to constant returns to scale, and both use the two factor inputs although with different intensities. Because perfect competition is assumed in both markets for commodities and factors, the production conditions of an economy can be summarised in the transformation curve (*AB*) shown in Fig. 1. Demand conditions are represented by community indifference curves (I, II, III, etc.), expressing a particular social welfare function for an unchanging distribution of income among the members of the community.[1] There are no transport costs.

Under these circumstances free trade permits an economy to operate with optimum technical efficiency in production

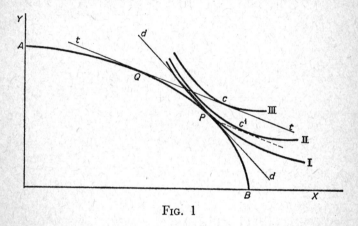

Fig. 1

and to maximise utility, subject to given constraints. This can be illustrated by reference to Fig. 1.

Without the opportunity to trade, the community produces and consumes at *P*, where the exchange ratio between the two commodities in production is equal to their rate of substitution in consumption as shown by the slope of the line *dd*. That is, the marginal rate of transformation in production (MRT) equals the marginal rate of substitution in consumption (MRS):

$$MRS = MRT_d.$$

[1] The use of community indifference curves has been criticised and justifying them involves very restrictive assumptions; for example, see Vanek [63] chap. 13.

17

The opportunity to trade is given by the international terms of trade between X and Y, the slope of the line tt. This permits the community to increase its welfare from I to III, by shifting production to Q (specialising more in production of Y) and shifting consumption to c, where according to Fig. 1 more of both X and Y are consumed:

$$MRS = MRT_d = MRT_f.$$

That is, the marginal rate of substitution between goods in consumption is equal to the marginal rate of transformation between goods in production, and in an open economy that includes transformation through international exchange.

Two components can be specified in the welfare gain. A consumption or exchange gain is represented by the shift from I to II (P to c^1) where the pre-trade output is exchanged for a superior consumption collection. A production or specialisation gain is represented by the shift from II to III, as a consequence of the move from P to Q; Q gives a more valuable combination of X and Y at international prices.

The essential argument for free trade, therefore, is that by permitting specialisation according to comparative advantage it optimises world trade, maximises world production and maximises world economic efficiency. Following the lines of modern welfare theory, free trade also allows the economy to maximise consumption utility, if those gaining from free trade can, at least, compensate losers by ideal lump-sum transfers involving no inefficiency or losses (see Samuelson [55]). The case for free trade, however, relies on otherwise utopian marginal conditions operating in the economic system in order to optimise world economic efficiency. Where other marginal conditions are not fulfilled only a 'second-best' optimum is possible and the removal of one constraint by establishing free trade need not result in an improvement in economic welfare.

THEORY OF SECOND BEST

The theory of second best was largely developed in the context of international trade by Meade [41]. It was generalised by Lipsey and Lancaster [37]. The general theorem for the second-best optimum states that if there is introduced into a general equilibrium system a constraint[1] which prevents the attainment of one of the Paretian conditions, the other Paretian conditions, although still attainable, are, in general, no longer desirable. Put another way, the theory of second best specifies that a situation in which more, but not all, of the Paretian optimum conditions are fulfilled is not necessarily, nor is it even likely to be, superior to a situation in which fewer conditions are fulfilled. Thus, although in a single general equilibrium system there is only one Paretian optimum, there are many possible combinations of constraints which give a second-best solution; there is no *a priori* way to decide between alternative situations without knowledge of the additional constraints and functional relationships within the model.

An example of second-best theory in the theory of tariffs may help to explain the concept. Lipsey and Lancaster cite the case of unilateral adoption of a free trade policy by one country in a many-country tariff-ridden world, which may actually result in lower real income not only in that country but in the world as a whole. Eliminating its own tariffs enables the country to equate the ratio of internal prices with international price ratios, but world demand and supply are distorted by other countries' tariffs so this is not a free trade world price relationship. The change may shift the internal price ratio closer to that in some other countries and away from that in others. On balance, therefore, the change may affect welfare or efficiency either by raising it, by lowering it, or by leaving it unchanged for the country removing tariffs and the world as a whole, depending on the nature of other constraints. Clearly, the discriminatory reduction of trade barriers in a customs union is an analogous case because it involves changes in trade patterns and leads to reallocations of resources inside and outside the customs union which may raise, lower or leave unchanged welfare in the countries forming the customs union and countries left outside.

[1] Constraints giving rise to second-best situations may be 'behavioural' (e.g. an unwillingness by entrepreneurs or workers to seek maximum returns) or 'policy-created' (e.g. taxes, subsidies, licences, etc.).

Development of the theory of second best has placed the theory of trade policy into the context of general equilibrium analysis. Adjusting trade policies at the margin involves substituting one type of distortion of Pareto optimality conditions for another, or the removal of one constraint in the presence of other constraints – the case with unilateral free trade mentioned above. Deciding between alternative policies involves a complex calculus based on comprehensive empirical information and knowledge of the functional relationships within the economic system.

EFFECTS OF TARIFFS

Before turning to an analysis of arguments for tariffs it is necessary to examine the effects of applying a tariff. An import duty may, of course, be an *ad valorem* or a *specific* levy; in some instances it may be imposed on a combined basis. Since a *specific* tariff is readily expressed as an *ad valorem* tariff (i.e. as a percentage of imported value), the discussion continues in these terms. In practice, of course, the effects of the alternative systems of levying the tariff may be different. For example, a *specific* tariff represents a higher *ad valorem* tariff on cheaper products than on dearer products, which may be especially important during periods of rising or falling prices.

A tariff is designed to penalise domestic consumers and foreign producers and to favour domestic producers and the Government. (It is equivalent to an excise tax on the consumer, the revenue from which is received by domestic producers in as far as they produce the imported good, with the residual accruing to the Government.) The manner in which this redistribution is achieved is best illustrated by means of partial equilibrium analysis for a single commodity X as shown in Fig. 2.

Demand for commodity X in country A is shown by the line D_A and domestic supply is shown by the line S_A. If we assume that there is no terms of trade effect (i.e. that the demand and supply for X in A do not affect world prices), then the supply of imports of X to A can be represented by

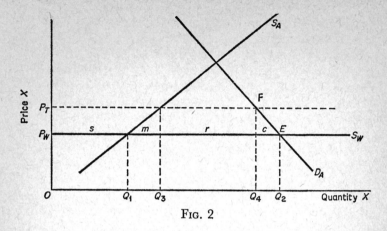

FIG. 2

$P_W S_W$; the supply of imports is infinitely elastic at price OP_W.

Thus, under conditions of free trade, the equilibrium market position for X is given by E. At a world free trade price of OP_W, total consumption is OQ_2, with OQ_1 supplied by domestic producers, and $Q_1 Q_2$ imported from foreign suppliers.

Suppose an *ad valorem* tariff of 30 per cent is introduced on imports of X. The price of X in A would then rise to OP_T, where $P_W P_T$ represents the tariff. Consumption of X declines to OQ_4 at the higher price, while domestic production increases to OQ_3. Imports decline to $Q_3 Q_4$. The changes caused by the tariff are best illustrated with the aid of Marshall's concept of consumers' surplus. Domestic producers of X increase their output and their sales revenue as a result of protection provided by the tariff (total sales $OQ_3 \times OP_T$ compared with $OQ_1 \times OP_W$). The increased revenue from sales is obtained partly at the expense of foreign suppliers ($Q_1 Q_3 \times OP_W$) and partly at the expense of domestic consumers' surplus ($s+m$); s represents higher profits earned at the higher price and larger output with tariff protection, and m is additional costs of increased domestic output. Domestic consumption is reduced by $Q_2 Q_4$ units of X, which involves a further loss to foreign suppliers of $Q_2 Q_4 \times OP_W$, and a loss of consumers' surplus equivalent to the area c. In addition, the Government receives tariff revenue shown by the area r (i.e. $Q_3 Q_4 \times P_W P_T$), which once more is

21

at the expense of consumers' surplus. Total consumers' surplus loss as a result of the tariff is represented by the area $P_T P_W E F$. Part of this, shown by s, is redistributed as producers' profits, and the Government collects r in tariff revenue.

The loss from protection, therefore, is represented in welfare terms by the two areas c and m; m represents the additional cost of domestic production of X under protection, and c represents the consumers' surplus loss caused by the price-increasing effect of the tariff. However, $(c+m)$ shows only the domestic loss caused by the tariff. Foreign suppliers suffer a loss of income $OP_W \times (Q_1 Q_3 + Q_4 Q_2)$, other things being unchanged.

Evidently, the protective loss from the tariff depends upon the slopes of the demand and supply curves in country A, and hence the elasticities of these curves in the vicinities of the prices before and after the tariff, assuming no effects on the terms of trade. If D_A were more steeply sloped through E, the loss of consumers' surplus c from the 30 per cent tariff would be much smaller, the decline in imports of X smaller also. Conversely, if the domestic supply curve S_A were sloped less steeply, the same 30 per cent tariff would have caused a much greater increase in domestic production, and a larger decrease in imports too.

TERMS OF TRADE EFFECTS

Imposition of a tariff raises the domestic price of the taxed commodity, which leads to a reduction in demand for imports of that commodity. If this represents a significant change in world markets it must result in a change in world prices, that is, in the terms of trade. In these circumstances domestic prices are not raised to the full extent of the tariff because part of the duty is borne by foreign suppliers (i.e. if $P_W S_W$ in Fig. 2 is upward-sloping). The analysis is only slightly modified by this, but changes in the terms of trade are most suitably examined in a general equilibrium model.

Consider Fig. 3, which employs Marshallian offer curves. (For an explanation of the derivation and properties of offer curves, see Leontief [36].) In a world with two countries, A and B, and two commodities, X and Y, OA represents the free trade offer curve of A, exporting X and importing Y. OB is the free trade offer curve of country B, exporting Y and importing X. Under conditions of free trade, the equilibrium rate of exchange between X and Y is shown by the slope of the line OP; only at this price are the two countries prepared to offer and receive the same amount of both commodities.

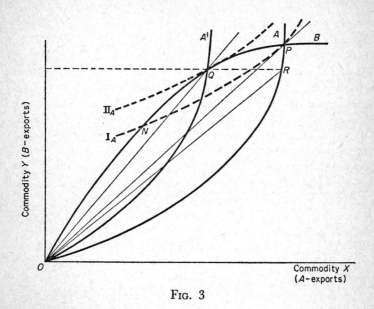

FIG. 3

Suppose country A imposes a 25 per cent *ad valorem* tariff collected in terms of the export X. This would have the effect of shifting A's offer curve to the left by one-fifth, indicating that a 25 per cent duty must be paid over to the Government on all imports. This imposition implies that for any given quantity of imports of Y, country A offers a smaller quantity of exports of X, the tariff being collected in terms of the export commodity X.[1] The effect of the tariff, therefore, would be to shift the

[1] Had the Government required payment of the tariff in terms of the imported commodity Y, the offer curve would have been shifted for a 25 per cent duty measuring vertically one quarter of

23

international terms of trade in favour of country A, since OQ is steeper than OP. The international price of Y in terms of X is shown by the slope of OQ, but the domestic price to consumers is greater, as shown by the slope of OR; the difference QR represents the tariff revenue. (Baldwin [5] has shown how the way in which the Government uses the tariff revenue also influences the position of the offer curve.)

If, instead of a foreign offer curve OB in Fig. 3, country A had been faced by an offer curve such as the straight line OP (i.e. an infinitely elastic foreign offer curve), the imposition of a tariff on imports of Y would not have affected the international terms of trade. This illustrates the situation postulated in the previous subsection, where the decline in A's imports as a result of a tariff did not affect the world market situation. A tariff can only improve a country's terms of trade, therefore, if the foreign offer curve is less than infinitely elastic.

THE OPTIMUM TARIFF

To show that a tariff can improve a country's terms of trade does not tell us anything about the overall welfare significance of the tariff. The introduction of trade extends the possible consumption opportunities facing a community which transposes its social welfare function (i.e. its family of community indifference curves). Meade [42] has developed the device of trade indifference curves which show equal social utility with trade. The severe restrictions associated with the use of community indifference curves still apply, including a constant distribution of income.

Refer again to Fig. 3. At the free trade price OP, there is one of A's trade indifference curves (I_A) passing through P at a tangent to the international price line OP (see Leontief [36]). This indifference curve cuts the offer curve OB at the

the distance between the horizontal axis X and all points on OA, and then adding this amount of commodity Y to the quantity of imports effectively demanded by the private sector. The tariff-distorted offer curve would then be to the right of OA^2 in Fig. 3. For a full discussion of tariff-distorted offer curves, see Vanek [63].

point N. If OB is elastic and country B does not retaliate against tariffs levied by country A, then a tariff levied by A which shifts its offer curve such that it cuts OB between P and N enables country A to achieve a higher trade indifference curve than the one through P. The optimum tariff, however, is that tariff which shifts OA to a position where it cuts B's offer curve at Q, where OB is tangent to an A indifference curve. Any tariff which shifts A's offer curve such that it cuts OB between N and P is a superior position compared with the free trade situation, but all are inferior to the tariff that shifts A's offer curve to a position passing through Q. Even this represents only a potential optimum, however, because any tariff affects income distribution. It will make some members of the community better off and others worse off. For an unambiguous increase in a country's welfare, therefore, the optimum tariff must be accompanied by a redistribution policy to compensate those who suffer under the tariff. As the optimum tariff increases total welfare, this redistribution is possible and some overall gain will remain.

Any tariff such that A's offer curve cuts OB to the left of N makes country A worse off than under free trade. The terms of trade are still greatly improved but the shrunken volume of trade makes A worse off. (For a comprehensive analysis of tariffs within a general equilibrium model using offer curves, see Vanek [63].)

An individual country is able to exert influence on the exchange ratio for its exports on world markets to the extent that there is any imperfection in the world market structure. Thus, unless the foreign offer curve (reciprocal demand curve) for a country's exports is infinitely elastic, a country must possess some monopoly in trade. This monopoly power to affect price is greater the more inelastic the demand for a country's exports.

The optimum tariff represents a 'first best' argument for a tariff, in that it produces an unambiguous gain in a country's welfare. Equalisation of foreign and domestic prices, under conditions of free trade, does not equate the domestic marginal rate of transformation in production and the domestic marginal rate of substitution in consumption (the internal equilibrium conditions) with the marginal rate of transformation through international trade. A suitable tariff, on the other hand, can bring these three marginal rates into equality by establishing an optimal situation for that economy. (If producers themselves within the tariff-levying country are able to exercise the monopoly power, there is no need for an optimum tariff policy to be applied. However, it is likely that the monopolists can extend this price distortion to domestic sales which would cause internal disequilibrium.)

So far it has been assumed that no retaliation takes place for the imposition of a tariff by country A. Clearly this is not realistic, and under normal circumstances one would expect country B to attempt to introduce its optimum tariff also. That is, in Fig. 3, country B applies a tariff such that its offer curve OB shifts until it cuts A's tariff-distorted offer curve OA^1 at an optimum position, where a B indifference curve is a tangent to OA^1. The terms of trade then move against A and in favour of B. Country A would be expected to retaliate by adjusting its tariff in order to seek an optimum position once more on B's tariff-distorted offer curve. And then B, and so on.

Even with retaliation permitted, however, Johnson [25] has shown that it is still possible for a country to gain by imposing an optimum tariff in spite of other countries following the same policy. He shows that a universally valid conclusion on optimum tariffs with retaliation is not possible and that the answer depends on the circumstances of particular cases.

ARGUMENTS FOR PROTECTION

Arguments for tariffs are diverse, often ingenious, and usually pressed by powerful groups in the community. Taxonomic discussions of the many types of argument for tariffs and other trade restrictions are to be found in many textbooks; see, for example, Meade [41], Haberler [23], Wells [67]. Limited space does not permit even the most popular arguments in favour of tariffs to be examined adequately here; the variety of presentations alone of the basic arguments would make this prohibitive. (Professor Johnson once classified arguments for protection under three headings: economic arguments, non-economic arguments and non-arguments!)

When considering a specific argument in favour of a tariff (or any other protective measure for that matter), it is worth remembering that a tariff can and usually does benefit some people within a community. It has been shown (Fig. 2) how a tariff enables domestic producers to raise their output and their profits on the protected commodity, which also increases or maintains the level of employment of certain resources specific to particular industries. Usually, such individual group interests are presented in terms of a much wider justification for tariffs as benefiting the whole community. What is good for one group is not necessarily good for the whole country, however, and it is the costs and benefits of a tariff for the whole community that must be considered.

DOMESTIC DISTORTIONS

For obvious reasons justification for a tariff is usually presented with regard to domestic considerations. The first concern should be with the effectiveness of a tariff as a remedy for the specified problem.

It has been established that the conditions of Pareto optimum are

$$\text{MRS} = \text{MRT}_d = \text{MRT}_f.$$

Therefore, the basic question is, where these conditions do not apply, can a tariff help to establish the equilibrium conditions?

Earlier (p. 25 above), it was shown that if a country has monopoly power in trade, the competitive free trade solution is characterised as

$$\text{MRS} = \text{MRT}_d \neq \text{MRT}_f.$$

If a suitable tariff is introduced – the optimum tariff – it is possible to achieve equality between price ratios of domestic and foreign producers, without destroying the domestic equality. In this case a tariff represents a first-best policy alternative for achieving optimum economic welfare.

27

Is it possible to achieve the same optimum conditions by means of a tariff in the face of domestic distortions?

$$\text{MRS} \neq \text{MRT}_d = \text{MRT}_f.$$

Introducing a tariff can equalise MRS and MRT_d, but it would destroy the equality between domestic and foreign producer prices. Bhagwati and Ramaswami [7], investigating this problem, establish that a tariff is, therefore, inferior to an optimum domestic tax and subsidy policy which eliminates the domestic inequality, without disturbing the external equilibrium.

The application of a tariff in the presence of domestic distortion is clearly an instance of the theory of second best. It involves the substitution of one deviation from optimum conditions ($\text{MRS} \neq \text{MRT}_d$) for another (disturbing $\text{MRT}_d = \text{MRT}_f$).

Johnson [28] examines these second-best arguments for protection under four groups:

   (i) arguments derived from immobility of factors and downward rigidity of factor prices;

  (ii) arguments derived from distortions in commodity markets;

 (iii) arguments derived from distortions in factor markets;

 (iv) the 'infant industry' argument.

Using the standard trade model, employed above to illustrate the benefits of free trade, Johnson shows in each of these four cases how the introduction of a tariff results in a suboptimal position, although if appropriately chosen it may result in welfare levels higher than under free trade. The first-best solution, however, involves a tax-cum-subsidy policy. For example, if the returns paid to a specified factor diverge in different industrial activities and represent a genuine distortion, an optimum situation can be achieved by subsidising the use of the factor by the sector which otherwise has to pay a higher price, or by taxing the use of the factor by the sector which otherwise has to pay a lower price; in either case the distortion is eliminated directly. Similarly, monopoly or oligopoly conditions in the production of a good have the effect of raising the price to consumers above the marginal cost of production. The argument for a tariff in this case is that the country gains by raising the price of imports above their world price, thereby compensating for the distortion that makes the price of domestically produced importables exceed their true social cost. Such a policy safeguards the monopolist's profits at the expense of a consumers' loss. The first-best remedial policy is to impose a tax-cum-subsidy measure to guide production into a situation where the marginal rate of transformation in domestic production is equal to the ratio of foreign prices.

Johnson concludes that although intervention through tariffs or export subsidies at appropriate levels may enable an improvement over the welfare level reached under free trade, it produces a suboptimal solution. Given the presence of domestic distortions, measures of trade protection lead to a decrease in welfare because a tariff involves a consumers' loss through a distortion of the domestic price ratio away from the international ratio. More particularly, if a tariff is used to achieve a specific production objective, the associated consumption effect of the tariff must involve a loss to consumers. Because the whole subject of tariff policy is an aspect of the theory of second best, it cannot be certain that a change in commercial policy leads to an improvement or a deterioration in the overall welfare conditions. It is concluded, therefore, that the only 'first best' economic argument for tariffs is the optimum tariff argument. All other arguments for protection of this kind are, in principle, arguments for some form of government intervention in the domestic economy. (The special case of 'infant industry' protection is discussed on p. 66 below.)

TARIFFS AND INCOME DISTRIBUTION

Redistribution of income resulting from a tariff intervention is illustrated in Fig. 2. In the long run, tariffs cause resources to shift from export industries (where comparative advantage exists) and into import-substitution activities, producing for home demand either in the protected industrial activities or in non-traded activities, where demand increases as a consequence of the consumption-tax effects of a tariff. This redirection of resources may be modified by the way in which the tariff revenue is spent by the Government. Eventually the effect of increasing tariffs is that the volume of trade diminishes and specialisation is reduced with ultimately unfavourable consequences for economic welfare.

Because the shape and position of a country's transformation curve (*AB* in Fig. 1) are determined by available resources and the production functions, it is possible to explore, in a limited way, the redistributive effects of a tariff on the economy. The Stolper–Samuelson theorem [58] demonstrates that in the context of the Heckscher–Ohlin model, with two factor inputs and two commodities, a move from a situation of no trade to free trade will reduce the return to a scarce factor in both relative and absolute terms. Hence a tariff, by raising the price of a commodity employing intensively the scarce factor, will benefit that factor at the expense of the other. The assumptions in this analysis are highly restrictive. As Pearce ([51] chap. 14) has explained, the assumption of only two commodities and two factors, the use of identical production functions in both countries and the neglect of demand effects in the theoretical model are crucial, and if these conditions are relaxed the outcome may be changed.

Evidently, opening an economy to free trade will reduce the return to a factor when it is relatively more abundant in other trading countries, and the Stolper–Samuelson theorem has been used to support the popular argument that a tariff protects the real wage of workers from ruinous competition of cheap foreign labour. Notice, however, that a country levying a tariff is impoverished compared with its position under free trade ($MRT_d = MRT_f$). Moreover, the terms of trade are likely to be altered by the tariff so that the domestic price of the protected commodity need not rise; if it does not, the return to the protected factor input would not rise. The use of a tariff to protect returns to one factor, say labour, is obviously a second-best situation; the case where a tariff is used to overcome domestic distortions caused by factor immobility or rigidities in factor prices is examined by Johnson [28].

30

The redistributive effects of a tariff in an economy can be far-reaching. Clearly the way in which a government chooses to spend the tariff revenue will affect prices of commodities and factors. In addition, aggregate expenditure patterns within the economy are directly affected. If there is an elastic demand for the good on which the tariff is levied, it reduces the total expenditure on that good, which means that expenditure on other items is raised (other things being unchanged). The result must be that prices and incomes alter. Alternatively, if demand is inelastic, total expenditure on a product on which the tariff is imposed is increased, which must cause cuts in expenditure elsewhere in the economy (other things being unchanged). Expenditure on substitutes and complements to the goods on which the tariff is levied is also disturbed. Obviously, therefore, the effects of a tariff can only be fully analysed within a general equilibrium model.

3 Non-tariff Distortions of Trade

As tariffs have been progressively reduced by multilateral agreements in GATT and by regional trade agreements such as EEC and EFTA, attention has focused more and more on other impediments to trade. Some non-tariff measures have been recognised and discussed for a long time; for example quotas, export subsidies and differences in industrial standards. Many other measures, however, either were not apparent or were considered to be of little consequence when tariffs were high. Following the very substantial reduction in tariffs agreed during the Kennedy Round negotiations and the increased significance of non-tariff barriers in EEC and EFTA now that industrial tariffs have been eliminated, these distortions of trade flows have developed into a major issue of commercial policy. In part the interest derives from a wish to extend trade liberalisation beyond tariff reductions, and in part because of the fear that non-tariff barriers may be substituted for tariffs removed according to international agreements.

The issue of non-tariff distortions of international trade is only one aspect of a much larger problem. Liberalisation of tariffs and other restrictions on industrial trade under the auspices of international organisations, together with the revolution in transport and communications, have facilitated a rapid increase in international economic interdependence. At the same time, however, national governments have adopted policies involving more active intervention in the pursuit of economic stability and full employment. More recently, as Ohlin points out [49], these policies have been extended in attempts to stimulate regional development, industrial adjustment, technological research and labour mobility. A contradiction has evolved, therefore, between these new responsibilities of governments and the general movement towards a more liberal international trading regime. The dilemma has been aggravated by inflexibilities in other economic variables, such as price and exchange-rate stability.

The significance of non-tariff distortions as an international policy issue is evident from the attention that has been given to studies undertaken in recent years by GATT, OECD, EEC and EFTA. Comprehensive lists have been compiled under separate headings for a wide range of measures and practices. Attempts to negotiate for the removal of the trade-distorting aspects of many measures, however, are likely to prove difficult owing to the specific domestic objectives that many such policies are designed to meet, quite apart from any protective effects they may have. Some non-tariff measures can be clearly shown to be for regulation of international trade, such as quotas, export subsidies and certain border charges. In many cases, however, the impact on international trade may be secondary to a domestic policy objective; regional development schemes, government procurement policies and most production subsidies appear to fall under this heading. Moreover, even in the former case, measures introduced to control trade flows may have been specifically chosen in the short run to overcome balance of payments difficulties, or to alleviate regional industrial adjustment problems simply because more conventional measures, such as raising tariffs and altering the exchange rate, are no longer acceptable. Mixed motives and the diffuse consequences of economic measures make the issue of non-tariff distortions of international trade a difficult area for negotiations. Measuring the impact of a specific measure on trade poses many difficulties. Furthermore, it is insufficient to examine most measures from the points of view of their trade-distorting effects alone. Firstly, the wider implications for the economy as a whole must be considered. Secondly, it is possible that an individual measure has been introduced to overcome another distortion, in which case its removal would create a new distortion. This interrelationship implies that all measures affecting trade flows must be included in an assessment.

Baldwin [4] defines a non-tariff trade-distorting policy as 'any measure (public or private) that causes internationally traded goods and services, or resources devoted to the production of these goods and services, to be allocated in such a way as to reduce potential real world income'. In a real world where any transaction is influenced by many pressures and economic policies, assessing the degree of interference caused by any one specific policy is a very difficult business. So far few attempts have been made to assess the impact of particular non-tariff measures on trade flows; in fact, the whole subject has hardly proceeded beyond the stage of classification and description.

CLASSIFICATION OF NON-TARIFF DISTORTIONS

Policies causing non-tariff distortions of international trade have been classified under various headings in surveys undertaken by international organisations. Detailed descriptions of different types of measure causing distortion of trade are available in the literature (Baldwin [4], Curzon [18]). In a survey of this kind it is not possible to discuss all types of distortion. Private restrictive practices causing distortions of trade are ignored because they are difficult to identify. This survey concentrates, therefore, on public sector distortions. A brief examination of the main types of barrier follows, according to the headings chosen by GATT for its classification of non-tariff distortions.

Government participation in trade

This category includes government procurement policies, state trading schemes, production and export subsidies and trade-diverting investments. Trade liberalisation has focused on consumption and production in the private sector, yet modern governments are large purchasers of goods and services in all countries. Many government purchasing agents and other public sector purchasers apply regulations which explicitly or implicitly discriminate against foreign suppliers. In most industrial countries only a very small proportion of total public expenditure is spent on imported goods. Baldwin [4] examines the regulations operating in particular countries.

One of the principal disadvantages faced by foreign suppliers is lack of information about tendering procedures. The EFTA countries have attempted to overcome this restraint by publishing a list of all major purchasing agencies in member countries; and a growing list of contracts going to suppliers in partner countries bears witness to its value. Progress towards international agreement to liberalise procurement policies in a wider context is likely to be slow. Government expenditures form an important element of government control over the domestic economy, and the social costs involved in allowing contracts to go to foreign suppliers could be considerable. In most cases distortions caused by discrimination in public procurement are secondary to their specific aims regarding regional policy, industrial adjustment, etc.

State trading monopolies represent a considerable obstruction to trade. In many cases they enjoy not only monopoly in the home market but also control imports and import prices. Examples include the National Coal Board in Britain, the Swedish alcohol monopoly and the French tobacco monopoly.

Export subsidies may be either general or applied to selective industries. For macro-economic purposes, such as improving the balance of payments or increasing employment levels, general export subsidies are used. Selective export subsidies may also improve the balance of payments, but normally they are expected to provide special economic assistance to particular industries. Both types of export subsidy can be introduced in a wide variety of ways. A common measure in recent years has been subsidised export credits. Direct export subsidies, such as the British export rebate scheme which operated from 1965 to 1967, have also been applied periodically for balance of payments reasons.

In many ways production subsidies overlap with export subsidies; indeed a domestic subsidy may be primarily directed at increasing exports. Usually domestic subsidies are directed towards achieving a particular policy objective at home and distortions of trade are incidental. But this is not always the case, and even where it is, the distortion of trade may still be

35

quite substantial. Common examples of production subsidies include regional development assistance, shipbuilding subsidies and price discounts for domestically used steel.

There is an interesting asymmetry in GATT's treatment of export subsidies and import duties. Whereas import duties are permitted, although subject to reduction by negotiation, export subsidies were outlawed from the outset. Yet the economic effects on the allocation of world resources of the two measures are symmetrical: import duties tend to shift resources towards the production of domestically consumed goods, export subsidies tend to divert resources towards foreign traded products. Baldwin [4] suggests that this implies in GATT 'that a country has a greater right to interfere with its own domestic markets than with the markets of other countries'. He also points out that GATT clearly favours producer interests over consumer interests.

Para-tariffs

This comprises a variety of measures which in their effects are very similar to tariffs. Systems of customs valuation and classification, discriminatory customs procedures and special charges made at the frontier clearly fall under this heading. Anti-dumping procedures, such as countervailing duties, are not specifically designed to distort trade, but sometimes such regulations are used protectively. All these types of measure raise the price of an imported product in the same way as a tariff.

Specific limitations on trade flows

This category comprises quantitative restrictions, licensing schemes, bilateral trade agreements and export restraints.

Quantitative restrictions are the most significant intervention. In most textbooks, quotas are treated in terms of their tariff equivalent.

In Fig. 2 (p. 21 above), imports of commodity X can be restricted to the quantity Q_3Q_4 either by imposing a quantitative restriction equivalent to Q_3Q_4 units, or by imposing a tariff P_WP_T which raises the domestic price from OP_W to OP_T, at which demand for imports equals Q_3Q_4. In practice, of course, this is only possible if the tariff-levying authority knows the domestic demand and supply curves as well as the foreign supply curves for the commodity, and authorities therefore tend to prefer to use quantitative restrictions (if permitted) as a more certain way of limiting imports to a particular volume.

Bhagwati [8] has shown that this equivalence proposition does not apply if perfect competition does not pertain, that is, where there are monopolistic elements in domestic production, or where there is not perfect competition among quota holders (e.g. where import licences are issued only to a few who enjoy a monopolistic position in the market). The difference between the free world import price and the domestic price in the presence of a quota, that is, the difference between OP_W and OP_T, shows the amount of profit per unit that the importer with a licence can obtain on the home market. If licences are auctioned, importers would be prepared to pay up to $P_W P_T$ per unit of import for permission to import.

Because quotas are considered to be more certain in their effects than tariffs, they are frequently chosen to restrict imports in times of slump, for example in the 1930s. During the 1950s, import quotas on industrial goods were removed by most industrial countries under agreements reached in OEEC and GATT. Quotas remained a popular device for restraining imports of agricultural goods, and their use has been extended in this field by some industrial countries in the course of the 1960s. More recently, quotas have been enjoying renewed popularity in connection with industrial trade too. The long-term arrangement regarding international trade in cotton textiles, negotiated in GATT in the early 1960s between major importing and exporting countries, represents a significant extension of quotas in the manufacturing field, although it does contain a growth element. Furthermore, some developed countries have negotiated 'voluntary' agreements with Japan and with some low-cost, less developed countries to regulate supplies of certain manufactured products. And following the same trend, strong pressures have emerged in the United States for imposing quantitative restrictions on a wide range of imports.

If reductions in tariffs are merely to be replaced by a more certain protective device, there has been little purpose to the whole tariff exercise in GATT. Quotas have always been permitted under GATT under special circumstances, such as where countries have faced balance of payments difficulties, or where there is a danger of market disruption from agricultural imports when domestic production is restricted. Failure to act against the illegitimate use of quotas to restrict agricultural trade under the latter exception appears to have encouraged wider resort to quotas and similar 'voluntary' agreements.

Restraints on imports and exports through prices

The most common interventions under this heading are prior deposit schemes, variable import levies, and various types of fiscal adjustments.

Import deposit schemes attempt to restrict imports temporarily by reducing the liquidity position of importers. By tying up funds in these deposits, the importer bears a cost in terms of lost earnings on these funds, as well as the constraint applied by reducing his general liquidity position. Prices of imported goods are likely to rise to meet part of the costs of the deposits, which will have an effect similar to a tariff. Variable levies are the main feature of the EEC's Common Agricultural Policy.

A considerable controversy has arisen recently over the problem of border tax adjustments for indirect taxes. Most countries levy taxes according to the destination principle; this means that exports are not taxed in the producing country but imports are taxed at the point of entry. GATT permits such adjustments for indirect taxes but not direct taxes, and thus encourages countries to use indirect taxes in preference to direct taxes for trade purposes, because a country that collects most of its revenue from direct taxes is unable to levy a compensating tax at the border on imports, or to refund taxes paid on exports. The underlying assumption is that indirect taxes are passed on in final prices whereas direct taxes are not. There is now little evidence to support it. Furthermore, changes in taxation, such as the harmonisation of EEC indirect taxes towards a value-added tax, introduce new types of border tax adjustments which create new distortions in international trade. (The effects of different types of selective indirect taxes and subsidies on trade flows are included in a study by Grubel and Common Johnson [22] of levels of effective tariff protection in the Market countries.)

Technical and legal regulations

The variety of measures under this heading are legion. They include sanitary regulations, health safeguards, industrial standards, labelling and packaging regulations and so on. If vigorously applied, these regulations can completely prohibit imports. These measures have provided significant barriers to trade in EEC and EFTA. In consequence, considerable attention has been given to harmonising certain industrial and technical standards; attempts are also being made to achieve co-ordination between the two organisations. Discussion of the detailed implications of such harmonisation can be found in Corbet and Robertson ([14] chaps 4-5).

ACTION ON NON-TARIFF DISTORTIONS

In the course of the Kennedy Round negotiations in GATT a number of important non-tariff distortions of trade were isolated. Except for the American Selling Price evaluation for benzonoid chemicals, which as a clear para-tariff is readily quantifiable and therefore negotiable, removal of which was made conditional by EEC and Britain for certain tariff reductions, little real progress was made on the issue. Nevertheless the raising of this issue has caused great interest in the whole subject of non-tariff distortions of trade flows. The danger now must be that countries will draw on the comprehensive lists that have been compiled by GATT and other organisations to find the most effective substitutes to protect industries from the effects of earlier tariff liberalisation. It has so far proved difficult to reach agreement to freeze the existing situation and prevent any new measures from being introduced. Until this is achieved, negotiations for liberalising non-tariff distortions must be difficult.

39

AGRICULTURAL TRADE

The special problems of world agricultural trade are most suitably mentioned under non-tariff barriers because tariffs, as such, play a relatively unimportant part in the protection maintained. Each developed country has its own distinctive set of agricultural policies which are complex both in themselves and in their effects. Developing countries whose produce competes with temperate agricultural produce suffer under these policies, and even producers of tropical produce face difficulties of trade preferences and established connections founded on former colonial links. The result is that the pattern of world trade in agricultural products is greatly distorted with marked discrimination against the most efficient suppliers.

The main aim of agricultural policies in most developed countries is to increase farmers' incomes. Secondary aims include stability of farm incomes, improvements in productive efficiency, strategic self-sufficiency and preservation of rural communities. To these ends countries have adopted policies of price support, import restrictions and export assistance. When considering international trade in agricultural produce, therefore, policies covering production cannot be treated separately from import or export policies. This makes trade negotiations in this field doubly complicated because any agreement must involve domestic policies to an extent which few countries are prepared to tolerate. In many cases domestic prices are fixed by agreement between the Government and farmers' representatives, and imports are then determined either by quotas, or tariffs fixed in relation to expected world prices at a level to equate import prices with the domestic price, or by a combination of tariffs and quotas. In addition, if surplus production occurs it is frequently exported with the aid of a subsidy, causing disruption in overseas markets. An extra protective measure which has been adopted in EEC's Common Agricultural Policy is the variable levy, which means that whatever the delivered price of foreign produce, the tariff is adjusted to ensure the domestic price cannot be undercut by more efficient producers. An alternative policy used in

Britain until now involves a more or less free market for local and foreign produce with a deficiency payment to British farmers to make up the difference between market prices and an agreed target price. Quotas have been progressively introduced into the British system in recent years, and in 1970 the Government announced its intention to shift towards a system of variable levies. (For a discussion of the differences between the British system and the EEC Common Agricultural Policy, see Josling [33] or Marsh and Ritson [40].)

During the last twenty years, when restrictions on trade in industrial goods have been progressively reduced under the general guidance of GATT, protectionism has been growing in agricultural trade. In the 1950s GATT failed to harness the major countries' agricultural policies to its regulations. Waivers granted at that time have been exploited, until they have apparently reached the ultimate in the EEC Common Agricultural Policy. Simultaneously, technological developments in farming have improved yields and raised output while effective demand has expanded more slowly, thus causing a growing disparity between farm and non-farm incomes which is at the centre of developed countries' agricultural policies. It creates a crucial social and political problem. These developments have interacted until now the situation in world agricultural markets has reached a crisis. Costly surpluses are being produced in countries with inefficient producers because of unrealistic pricing policies; and efficient low-cost producers are facing severe competition in some markets from exports of these surpluses backed by enormous subsidies. The chaos created by these protectionist policies is likely to be a major policy issue in the 1970s (see, for example, Coppock [13] and Fernon [20]). Moreover, if the protectionist trend is not reversed, there is a danger that it will spill over into increased protectionism for industrial goods. Already the United States and other agricultural exporters have stated that any further steps to liberalise industrial trade must be conditional on introducing an orderly market for agricultural trade and reducing protectionism.

4 Measuring the Effects of Trade Policy

A major problem for policy-makers is to estimate the effectiveness of alternative trade policy measures in order to find the most efficient selection for the achievement of a particular policy objective. Discussion of the effects of tariffs has shown already that the height of a tariff offers little guidance as to its restrictiveness, which depends also on demand and supply characteristics in the relevant markets. The protective effects of many non-tariff measures are even more difficult to assess.

Tariffs have received most attention in attempts to evaluate protection, because of their dominance in commercial policy. Practical concern to bring down tariff levels by means of tariff bargaining in GATT and negotiations for regional trade agreements have, despite the theoretical warnings, put most emphasis on comparing the height of tariffs in industrial countries. In such comparisons two procedures have been generally adopted: the calculation of weighted and unweighted averages. Under the first alternative, duties on individual commodities are often weighted by the value of imports into the country in question, but this has been shown to give distortions; low duties associated with high levels of imports are given large weights, whereas high duties that restrict imports have low weights. Alternative weighting systems have included values in domestic consumption or production and values in world trade, but each has its drawbacks; for a review of the relevant literature, see Balassa [2]. The alternative of unweighted averages is most commonly used, therefore, to avoid these distortions. But even then, the range of tariffs levied on individual items within a product group can still give rise to controversies, as illustrated by the 'disparities issue' in the Kennedy Round [1] when it was claimed that a 50 per cent cut on a high tariff represented a smaller concession than a 50 per cent cut on a low tariff.

Tariffs, and many other protective measures, are designed to protect domestic industry from foreign competition by creating divergences between the relationships of commodity prices in international markets and those in domestic markets. The price differences discourage consumption expenditure on items made more expensive by tariffs, while they encourage domestic resources to shift into industries favoured by protection. As long as all output consists of final goods produced entirely from primary resource inputs – labour, capital and land – these consumption and production effects of a tariff are readily demonstrated. Once the existence of intermediate products is recognised, however, the protective effect depends on the structure of production and the costs of intermediate inputs, including the effects of tariffs and other trade restrictions. Consumption of a protected item still depends on its final price to consumers and the price-responsiveness of the demand schedule. Productive resources are attracted into a protected activity in so far as that industry can attract resources away from other employments by offering higher returns. And since a product's final value is the sum of primary production costs plus the costs of intermediate inputs, the extent to which higher returns can be offered to primary resource inputs depends on the difference between the change in costs of intermediates induced by trade-distorting measures and the change in the final value of a product caused by protective measures, in this case a tariff.

In order to allow for the influence of intermediate production, the concept of the 'effective rate of protection' has been evolved. It has been applied principally to tariffs, and it will be discussed in that way here, but it can be extended to include non-tariff distortions.

EFFECTIVE TARIFF RATES

Corden [15, 16] defines the effective protective rate as 'the percentage increase in value added per unit in an economic activity which is made possible by the tariff structure relative to the situation in the absence of tariffs but with the same exchange rate'.

This is best illustrated by means of a numerical example. Suppose a product F can be imported under free trade conditions at a price of 100. Let the cost of intermediate inputs be 50. Then, under free trade conditions, the value added in the final stage of producing F is $100 - 50 = 50$. If a 10 per cent tariff is introduced on imports of F, the domestic price of F increases to 110. Assuming there is no change in cost of intermediates, the value added in the final production process of F is increased to 60 $(110 - 50)$. The effective rate of protection is $\left(\dfrac{60 - 50}{50}\right) = 20$ per cent. Thus a 10 per cent nominal tariff levied on the price of the final product F represents an effective rate of protection on that process of 20 per cent.

Presented in terms of domestic value added in an industry and value added under free trade conditions, the effective rate of protection is a rather awkward calculation. Corden [15, 16] and Johnson ([29] chap. 12) have evolved a much simpler presentation using a unit cost approach:

$$
e = \frac{t_j - \sum\limits_{i=1}^{n} a_{ij}\, t_i}{1 - \sum\limits_{i=1}^{n} a_{ij}}
$$

where e_j = effective protective rate for activity j
$\quad\quad t_j$ = nominal tariff rate on j
$\quad\quad t_i$ = nominal tariff rate on i $(i = 1, \ldots, n$ inputs)
$\quad\quad a_{ij}$ = share of input i in cost of j in absence of tariffs.

(Note that the effective protective rate does not depend on inputs to its inputs; any effects from tariffs on earlier stages in production are included in the cost of the inputs.) This formula allows complicated examples involving tariffs on several inputs to a process to be calculated with ease, as long as the share of each input in the value of final output from a process is known.

Suppose in the example of product F, used earlier, a tariff of 5 per cent is introduced on the only intermediate input, which represents one-half of the final value of F in the absence of tariffs. The cost of the intermediate input rises to 52·5 $\left(=50 \times \frac{105}{100} \right)$. With the nominal tariff on F unchanged, value added in the final processing of F decreases from 60 to 57·5 $(=110-52·5)$. So the effective protective rate of F declines from 20 per cent to 15 per cent $\left(\frac{60-52·5}{50} \right)$, the tariff on the intermediate input raises its cost to domestic users and, *ceteris paribus*, the value added in F declines.[1]

Having recognised that import duties affect resource allocations, it is evident that other measures also affect the costs of inputs and outputs in a similar fashion. An export subsidy has the same effect on domestic prices as a tariff. Commodities receiving an export subsidy become more expensive at home as output is diverted towards overseas markets. (The traditional assumption of perfect competition in international trade means that if a commodity is exported it cannot be simultaneously an import, and vice versa.) Hence, it acts in the same way as a tariff and raises the effective protective rate of the subsidised activity. If this output is used as an intermediate input to another process, its higher cost reduces the effective protective rate of the higher-stage process. Conversely, both an export tax and an import subsidy encourage home consumption of a product in question and reduce its effective protective rate. If used as an intermediate input to a higher stage of production, then input costs are lowered and the effective protective rate raised on the output.

TRADE EFFECTS OF DOMESTIC TAXES

Traded goods are also affected by internal taxes and subsidies on production and consumption. General taxes, such as

[1] Introducing the same information into the Corden formula gives

$$e_f = \frac{·10-(·50 \times ·05)}{1-·50} = \frac{·10-·025}{·50} = \frac{·075}{·50} = 15 \text{ per cent.}$$

income tax, profits tax and value-added tax, do not interfere with the internal allocation of resources since their effect is uniform for a particular type of primary resource input. Indirect taxes which have different incidence, however, can affect the allocation of resources.

Excise taxes levied according to the destination principle do not affect the effective protective rates for taxed goods, because they are applied equally to imports and domestic substitutes, while exports are not taxed. If a product bearing an excise tax is used as an intermediate input, however, the effective protective rate on that process is reduced because input costs are raised by the tax. (This can, of course, convert a positive nominal tariff into a *negative* effective rate of protection.)

Taxes are not generally levied on the origin principle, but production subsidies are often distributed according to the origin principle. As long as imports of competing products continue, a production subsidy does not affect the domestic price, although domestic output is encouraged. The effective protective rate of the subsidised product is, therefore, raised by the subsidy. Processes using the subsidised product as an intermediate input continue to pay the same costs so that their effective protective rates are unchanged.

Grubel and Johnson [22] and Barker and Han [6] have demonstrated that when indirect taxes are taken into account, the effective rates of protection from a given list of nominal tariffs are substantially modified. They show that for the EEC countries in 1959, and for Britain in 1963, much lower effective rates of protection were provided by tariffs if indirect taxes were included in the calculation.

NON-TARIFF DISTORTIONS

One feature of the concept of effective protection is that any selective measure that affects input or output prices can be introduced into the formula. (For example, a quota has the same results on effective rates of protection as an equivalent tariff.) Baldwin [4] has attempted to measure the effective protective rates provided by some non-tariff measures on particular commodity groups in the United States and Britain. He shows that the average level of effective protection given to industry in both countries by tariffs and other measures is much greater than that suggested by nominal tariffs alone: protection from non-tariff devices is shown to have increased both relatively and absolutely for all commodity groups. Baldwin concludes that it is essential to consider all measures that distort trade patterns when calculating effective protection.

RESOURCE ALLOCATION

Measured in the manner described, the effective protective rate represents the maximum percentage increase in value by primary resources during a production process that is made possible by the tariff. The underlying assumptions establish this. Following traditional trade theory, it is assumed that primary resource inputs are available in fixed quantities and are immobile between countries, that full employment is maintained by means of suitable fiscal and monetary policies, and that all tariffs, taxes and subsidies are applied in a non-discriminatory manner. Another condition is that physical input–output coefficients are fixed and that they can be expressed in terms of the final cost of production. The elasticities of demand for all exports and the elasticities of supply for all imports are considered infinite. Hence, although a tariff protects production, any increase in demand for imported intermediate inputs into that process is met without any change in their costs. Similarly, increased exports can be sold abroad without reducing their prices on world markets. Finally, in order to maintain an established relationship between foreign prices and domestic prices, it is assumed that all traded goods continue to be traded even after changes in trade policy.

If industrial activities are ranked according to their effective rates of protection, then primary resources would tend to be attracted, by the prospect of receiving higher rewards, into activities with the highest protective rates and away from the least protected or negatively protected activities and from non-traded activities.[1] This movement of resources is modified by the pattern of consumption expenditure. Consumption shifts away from goods with high nominal tariffs and towards goods with low nominal tariffs and non-traded goods, subject to price-sensitivity of demand patterns. Ultimately it is the interaction of these two influences that determines the allocation of resources and the distribution of expenditure in the economy.

The effective protective rate is not a perfect device for indicating the way in which primary resources are likely to shift in response to trade restrictions. If any of the fixed conditions (specified above) change, the actual value added can fall below the potential given by the effective rate of protection. In practice, therefore, protective effects are more complex. In large countries or trading blocs, such as EEC, the assumption of complete elasticity of supply of imported inputs does not hold. As the simple assumptions underlying this approach are qualified, the concept of effective protection becomes more difficult to calculate because it requires comprehensive general equilibrium analysis.

Controversy has arisen about some fundamental aspects of the theory of effective protection, and these were revealed fully during a conference held at GATT in 1970 (see Grubel and Johnson [69]).

EMPIRICAL STUDIES

The study of effective tariff rates explains why an escalated structure of tariffs is necessary if protection on higher stages of production is to be greater than on earlier stages. If higher

---

[1] So far it has been assumed that all goods are traded, but some production (e.g. public utilities and most services) does not enter international trade. Such activities are nevertheless influenced by the tariff structure, either indirectly through consumption patterns, or directly where they are used as inputs in the production of traded goods (see Corden [15]). Treatment of non-traded goods in empirical studies has given rise to controversy (compare Balassa [2] and Corden [15]).

tariffs are levied on material inputs than on final output, for example, it is quite possible that a positive nominal tariff represents a negative rate of effective protection. The observed escalation of tariff structures in most developed countries means that tariff structures are biased in favour of imports of materials and against imports of processed products; this imposes especially heavy barriers against processed goods in which less developed countries have comparative advantage and relegates them to supplying primary commodities (see Balassa [2]).

All empirical studies show that effective tariffs exceed nominal tariffs. In some cases this influences the country ranking of tariffs of individual countries; Balassa [2] found that Britain, the EEC and Japan were less restrictive compared with other countries in terms of effective tariffs than in terms of nominal tariffs. These revisions are caused by differences in tariff structures; countries with relatively higher tariffs on intermediate inputs or raw materials have less protection on higher stages in production. This has important applications in bargaining for tariff cuts; for example, a cut in the duty on an intermediate product is likely to increase imports of this item, but by raising the level of effective protection on output using this input this may be more restrictive of trade. This emphasises the need to consider the whole structure of tariffs and other restrictive measures in order to assess the effects of protection on an economy.

5 Regional Trade Groupings

The creation of regional trade groupings is an aspect of international trade policy that has been vigorously pursued in the last two decades. A fundamental principle of GATT is that there should be no discrimination in the trade policy measures applied to imports of the same commodity from different sources. (In fact, it proved necessary to allow preference agreements existing when GATT was established in 1947 to continue; under Article 1, however, they could not be increased, and hence, as tariffs have been reduced, margins of preference have diminished.) Article 24 provides the only grounds on which new discriminatory arrangements can be established in the form of customs unions and free trade areas. According to Article 24 such agreements should lead to the complete removal of restrictions 'on substantially all trade' between the member countries, 'within a reasonable period of time' and without increasing the general level of protection against third countries. The founders of GATT permitted these discriminatory agreements in the belief that the removal of restrictions on mutual trade among a group of countries represented a movement towards free trade. Subsequent work on the theory of second best, however, has demonstrated that a partial movement towards free trade by the elimination of trade barriers among a restricted group of countries, which appears to fulfil more, but not all, of the (Paretian) optimum conditions, is not necessarily, nor is it even likely to be, superior to a situation in which fewer conditions are fulfilled (see Lipsey and Lancaster [37]).

Regional trade agreements, besides by-passing the principle of non-discrimination, also attribute greater emphasis to reciprocity, which is the second fundamental principle of GATT. Countries dissatisfied with the rate of progress of multilateral negotiations for reciprocal reductions in trade restrictions on a most-favoured-nation basis are able to join together in limited agreements to suit their collective interests. The six EEC countries, whose attempts to accelerate the removal of trade restrictions in GATT in the 1950s were frustrated, eventually resorted to Article 24 and drew up the Treaty of Rome. Other groups of countries have since compacted regional agreements.

The establishment of regional trading agreements has helped to sustain the momentum of multilateral negotiations for the liberalisation of trade. The experiences of EEC and EFTA in removing tariffs so painlessly demonstrated that tariffs were much less important than many governments considered them to be twenty years ago. More immediately, the threat of discrimination by the EEC countries against imports from third countries stimulated two initiatives in GATT for new rounds of negotiations for tariff reductions in the 1960s: the Dillon Round and the Kennedy Round. And success with linear tariff reductions in the two European trading blocs was instrumental in the decision to revise the negotiating technique in the Kennedy Round from the traditional item-by-item approach to an across-the-board linear cut in all tariffs.

Economic integration may be defined as the process by which discontinuities and discriminations existing along national frontiers are progressively removed between two or more countries. It is customary to classify various stages of the integration process according to the extent of the discrimination removed, which gives the following stages:

  (i) the free trade area, which implies the elimination of tariffs and other restrictions on trade between members, while retaining independence of commercial policy against third countries;

 (ii) the customs union, which in addition unifies the tariffs and trade policies of member countries against outsiders;

(iii) the common market, where all restrictions on factor movements within the area are also abolished;

(iv) the economic union, where economic, monetary, fiscal and social policies are harmonised.

Two comments must be made about this kind of classification. First, it is only intended to assist discussions. Actual regional agreements are unlikely to fit exactly into these simple categories. Second, the different categories should not be interpreted as stages in a movement towards full economic union. They may represent stages in a continuous process but they can just as well be ends in themselves. It is not inevitable that embarking on a free trade area must necessarily lead on to more advanced forms of integration, although additional benefits may accrue from the harmonisation of national economic policies.

THEORY OF CUSTOMS UNIONS

The theory of customs unions may be defined as that branch of tariff theory which deals with the effects of geographically discriminatory changes in trade barriers. Pursued almost exclusively in static terms, this body of analysis is concerned with the allocation of resources under the normal restrictive assumptions found in traditional trade theory – perfect competition, no transport costs, no economies of scale, etc. Most analysis is under partial equilibrium conditions. Although general equilibrium models have been attempted, they are very complex in structure (see Vanek [64]).

Study of the effects of customs unions has been confined mainly to the welfare gains and losses resulting from the exploitation of comparative advantage by means of trade following a change in levels of protection. Limited attention has been given also to gains from terms of trade effects and the effects of economies of scale associated with the creation of larger markets.

The nature of the theory of customs unions, however, has meant that three very important practical questions have received hardly any theoretical consideration. First, what welfare gains, or losses, may result from changes in the rate of economic growth associated with the creation of a customs union? Second, does increased foreign competition introduced by the discriminatory removal of trade restrictions effect improvements in levels of technical efficiency? Third, what measures are necessary to facilitate adjustments in member economies during the transition phase in order to achieve potential benefits from the customs union? Theory offers very little guidance to policy-makers concerned with these vital questions.

Viner [65] was the first to show that a customs union does not necessarily represent a movement towards a free trade optimum situation, since it combines elements of free trade with elements of greater protection. In so far as the mutual removal of tariffs among members leads to the displacement of high-cost domestic production by lower-cost output from the partner country there is *trade creation*, which raises economic welfare by improving the allocation of resources within the union and for the world as a whole. A less efficient allocation of resources results, however, where higher-cost supplies from a partner country replace low-cost imports from third-country producers. This *trade diversion* leads to a welfare loss. The net balance of these two effects determines the overall impact of a customs union on its members. It follows that if two countries forming a customs union do not produce any similar products, there can be no opportunity for trade creation, although substantial trade diversion is possible. Lipsey [38], in an excellent survey of customs union theory, summarised by saying that 'a customs union is more likely to bring gain, the greater is the degree of overlapping between the class of commodities produced under tariff protection in the two countries'.

In his model, Viner emphasised production effects. He was interested in the location of production under conditions of constant costs, and he assumed that commodities were consumed in fixed proportions. When prices change, however, consumers tend to substitute a cheaper product for more expensive products. Hence, it is necessary to consider not only production effects but also consumption effects caused by changes in protection following the formation of a customs union.

When consumption effects are introduced, Michaely [45] demonstrates that even trade diversion does not automatically lead to a reduction in welfare. If the price of a product imported from a partner country after the union is established is less than the price of the same product imported from a third country inflated by the tariff, then the discriminatory removal of the tariff can improve economic welfare in the importing country, even though production is less efficient under these circumstances. (This assumes that the tariff revenue lost is not recouped by the Government raising a new tax, which would complicate the assessment.) Michaely concludes that trade diversion is less likely to lead to a welfare loss, the smaller the difference in production costs beween partner-country suppliers and third-country suppliers, and the higher the initial tariff levied by the importing country and the higher the tariff preference granted to partner producers after the union is established. (With production under conditions of rising costs, the margin of gain from trade diversion is smaller, *ceteris paribus*, because as imports from the partner suppliers increase, their costs rise, while as demand for third countries' output diminishes their costs fall.)

The aim of a tariff is to raise domestic output of the protected good, but it also reduces domestic consumption through higher prices. Similarly, the removal or reduction of a tariff has a production effect, that is, output in the tariff-levying country declines, and a consumption effect, whereby at lower prices more of the commodity is consumed. Meade [43] and Johnson [25] have both elaborated the theory of customs union in terms of consumption and production effects for trade creation and trade diversion, within a model with rising costs. Fig. 4 illustrates this analysis under partial equilibrium conditions.

The line D_A represents the demand curve for product X in country A. S_A shows the rising cost supply curve of output of the domestic industry in A. S_{A+B} shows the total supply curve for domestic production in A plus exports from the partner country B to A after formation of a customs union. To eliminate terms of trade effects, it is assumed that country A does not account for a significant share of world demand; consequently world supply can be represented by $P_W S_W$. Clearly, according to the diagram a tariff is necessary for product X to be produced at all in country A.

If a tariff of $P_W Q$ is levied by A, then total consumption is ON, composed of LN imports from the lowest-cost world supplier

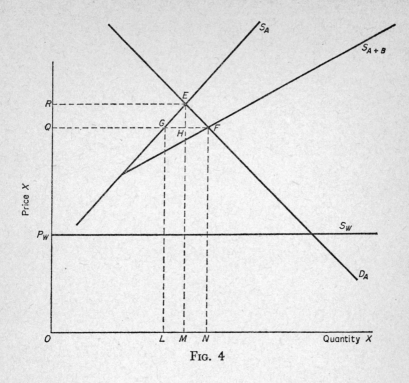

FIG. 4

at price P_W plus domestic production OL. After a customs union is formed between A and B the total consumption in A remains at ON, provided the tariff against third countries remains at the initial level. Production in A remains at OL, but imports now come from the partner country B, against whose products the tariff is no longer levied. This represents pure trade diversion. (If a tariff of less than $P_W Q$ is levied against third countries after the union is formed, then in addition there is a tariff reduction effect as well as trade diversion. Some imports from the rest of the world continue and production in A declines.)

Supposing A levied an initial tariff of $P_W R$, or more, this would provide complete protection of the home market. That is, total consumption is equal to domestic production at the point E. A customs union between A and B with a tariff against third countries of at least $P_W Q$ would lead to a new equilibrium point at F. This illustrates pure trade creation,

55

composed of a consumption effect, the increase in consumption from OM to ON, and a production effect LM representing the decline in high-cost production in A and its replacement by imports from B. The total welfare gain in this is shown by the area of the triangle EGF. The area EHF would be the gain in consumers' surplus; the area EHG would represent a reduction in costs of producing X. The area $RQGE$ represents a transfer from domestic producers' surplus to consumers' surplus.

If the initial tariff levied by A is somewhere between $P_W Q$ and $P_W R$, then both trade diversion and creation are present. Provided the tariff against third countries remains at least $P_W Q$, the equilibrium is at F and the consumption and production effects can be shown to be represented by triangles smaller than EHF and EHG in the previous case.

Trade creation, therefore, is composed of a production effect, which is the replacement of high-cost domestic production by cheaper imports of the same goods from partner countries, and a consumption effect, involving the substitution of low-cost partner production for domestic production. Similarly, trade diversion has two aspects: an increase in the cost of identical goods owing to a shift from third-country to partner sources, and substitution of higher-cost partner goods for lower-cost third-country supplies as a result of the discriminatory tariff cut. In addition, imports from partner countries may expand as a result of new expenditure made possible by higher real income achieved through resources saved by the formation of a customs union. Thus, there are three effects on trade flows: a substitution effect between producers, a substitution effect between goods, and an income effect.

The terms of trade effects of a customs union may also be important and may involve further increases in real income for members. Trade diversion means that the value of trade with third countries is likely to diminish. Other things being equal, therefore, one would normally expect prices of imports into the customs union to fall, while prices of exports from the customs union would remain unchanged or would rise. A favourable movement in the terms of trade would result in the short run. (Secondary effects in third countries might lead to some amelioration if their demand for exports from the customs union declines.) The change in the terms of trade depends on the size of the customs union and the elasticity of the offer curves of the union members and the rest of the world (see Vanek [63] chap. 18). In the long run, of course, the terms of trade of the customs union are determined in accordance with all the adjustments resulting from the completion of the customs union.

Certain general principles emerge from this examination of the trade effects of a customs union. First, a country is more likely to gain from trade creation in a customs union, the higher the initial level of its tariffs and the greater the elasticity of its domestic demand for the supply of goods which the partner country can produce. Second, a country is less likely to lose from trade diversion, the smaller the initial differences in costs between the partner and foreign sources of supply for goods which both can produce, i.e. the more elastic is the partners' supply and the less elastic is the foreign supply. Third, a country is more likely to gain on its terms of trade with foreign countries the more inelastic is the foreign supply of imports to it and the more inelastic the foreign demands for its exports. Moreover, the lower is the common external tariff established by the customs union, the smaller is likely to be the loss from trade diversion, although similarly the terms of trade movements are less favourable with regard to third countries.

MEASURING THE TRADE EFFECTS OF A CUSTOMS UNION

When measuring the actual effects of integration on trade flows there are two basic problems to be resolved. The first is to estimate the extent to which trade between participating countries is greater than it would have been in the absence of the customs union. In order to isolate the specific effects of a customs union agreement, however, it is necessary to eliminate the influence of other changes affecting trade that occur during the period of its establishment. For example, trading relationships between members of a union and outsiders are affected

57

by changes in trade policy negotiated in GATT and other international institutions, or undertaken unilaterally, and changes in the commodity composition of world trade may also influence trade changes within the union. In addition, there are changes as a result of forming a customs union that affect trade patterns: adjustments to a common external tariff cause some members to raise tariffs against outsiders while other members reduce their tariffs (this is sometimes referred to as 'external trade creation', and may be positive or negative); maintaining balance of payments equilibrium after joining a customs union may require changes in external economic policy too, which will affect trade with partner countries and outsiders.

Once an estimate of the trade effects of a customs union is obtained, the second problem is to estimate how far this increase in trade involves trade creation and how far it is due to trade diversion. Several attempts have been made to measure the trade effects of the creation of the EEC and EFTA. Useful surveys of these empirical studies are available in Lundgren [39], Balassa [3] and the EFTA Secretariat's study [19].

Two main types of approach can be identified in the empirical studies of the EEC and EFTA so far undertaken. The first involves measuring changes in trade shares. For example, shares of intra-area imports in total imports by the constituent countries are compared with the share of imports from third countries in the same total over a period of years. Over any period of years long enough to reveal the effects of tariff removal in a customs union, however, many other factors influencing trade are likely to change, and discounting their effects is a difficult process; see, for example, GATT [21]. Another drawback is that this approach does not allow the total actual increase in trade (what Balassa calls 'gross' trade creation [3]) to be divided into trade diversion and trade creation, as theory requires if the welfare effects are to be evaluated.

The second approach attempts to get round the difficulties by relating changes in imports to the development of demand. (No empirical studies have taken much account of supply factors, which evidently can help to explain observed changes in trade flows.) Balassa [3] uses a method based on the income

58

elasticity of import demand (i.e. the ratio of the average annual rate of change of imports to the average annual rate of change of GNP). This approach implies that union members' elasticities of import demand would not change in the absence of the tariff changes and that the commodity pattern of demand is unchanging. Trade diversion is shown by a fall in income elasticity of demand for imports from outsiders; 'gross' trade creation is indicated by a rise in the income elasticity of demand for imports from partner countries.

The EFTA study [19] uses domestic demand (output less exports plus imports) for each commodity as a demand variable. Trends in trade among the member countries in the pre-union period, 1954–8, are extrapolated into the period 1959–65, and these estimates are compared with the actual trade between the member countries in the latter period. Trade diversion is established if imports of commodities from non-EFTA sources are less than projected; trade creation is measured inasmuch as actual imports from EFTA partners exceed the projected values. This approach involves some heroic assumptions about past trends continuing in the future and the data used to establish trends can be crucial, especially as regards base dates. A similar approach is used by Truman [60] in a study of the trade effects of the EEC for the period 1954–64.

Empirical studies of the trade effects of the EEC and EFTA show quite substantial increases in intra-trade compared with estimates of trade flows in the absence of these regional agreements. Results of different studies show wide variations, but in 1967 intra-trade in both groups was probably 60 per cent higher than it would have been. When these trade effects are translated into gains in terms of GNP or some other measure of welfare, however, they are found to represent a very small gain; all estimates give a result less than 1 per cent of GNP for the group of participating countries (see Lundgren [39]).

INDIRECT EFFECTS OF CUSTOMS UNIONS

The meagre results obtained from empirical studies of the impact of customs unions based on traditional theory have caused many proponents of integration to suggest other sources of economic benefit. These are often popularly referred to as the 'dynamic advantages', and include economies of scale, the effects of increased competition and opportunities for faster economic growth. In fact, these effects can be divided into 'once-for-all' changes and genuine dynamic effects involving continuing adjustments over time. The former can be examined in terms of the type of static analysis already employed to consider trade effects.

Increased specialisation within a customs union leads to the expansion of output in efficient activities, which introduces opportunities for additional economies of scale: see Scitovsky [56] and Meade [43]. But pre-union tariffs represent a significant barrier to the exploitation of such economies only if the decline in costs from these economies is less than the tariff, in which case the gains are probably quite small. If the gains were greater than the initial tariff, then the failure to achieve them must emanate from other factors in the pre-union situation, such as political risk or insufficient market information.

Considerable emphasis has been given to the subject of economies of scale in recent discussion of enlargement of the European Economic Community. Some commentators see substantial opportunities for reductions in costs in Britain Swann [59], Pinder [52]) from access to larger markets. Other writers, however, point out that there is little theoretical support for such statements. Lundgren [39] asks how, if the tariff effects of a customs union are small, as empirical studies suggest, can tariffs succeed in preventing firms from already enjoying the economies of scale in large part? It has also been pointed out that Britain already has free or preferential access to markets of more than 150 million in EFTA and the more developed Commonwealth countries. It is difficult to believe that many economies of scale can be found beyond this size of home market, and the rapid development of world trade in manufactures indicates that remaining tariffs are surmountable barriers. In certain high-technology industries, such as aircraft, computers and electronics, economies of scale in research and development expenditure may be significant, but in these

60

sectors tariffs and other trade restrictions are of little importance. Government co-operation is the key to economies of scale in these sectors, which goes beyond normal customs union theory.

Closely linked with arguments for economies of scale from customs unions are the advantages from increased competition; high levels of protection allow inefficient methods of production to persist when greater efficiency is possible. In some industrial sectors, the optimum plant size is such that most national markets can only support one or two separate firms. Removal of trade barriers, therefore, by increasing competition in the larger market, favours the most efficient firms, which results in lower production costs overall. Less efficient firms within the union must either improve their production processes in order to compete with the most aggressive firms, or they are driven from the industry by the more efficient producers.

Greater competition and new opportunities for economies of scale, therefore, may lead to changes in production methods which bring greater efficiency in addition to the gains from specialisation. Whether these changes can greatly enhance the observed gains from the trade effects of a customs union is open to some doubt; very little research has been undertaken to measure the effects of changes in production methods induced by regional trade agreements.

Improved allocation of resources and greater specialisation in production in a customs union, supplemented by economies of scale and increased competition, result in a once-for-all increase in total output and income, provided full employment is maintained. Once the necessary economic adjustments have taken place, however, such as switching resources and investment in new plant to exploit new opportunities in the larger market, if there is no further change the rate of economic growth may return to its original level, although the total output is higher so that the absolute value of economic growth each year is higher. A higher rate of economic growth can only be sustained if a continuing change in economic variables occurs, such as an enduring higher rate of investment or a general upward shift in businessmen's expectations. Both these are possible in the changed circumstances of a customs union. Expectations change not only because of new trading conditions but also from increased knowledge made available to consumers, producers and governments from the publicity, discussion and general ballyhoo surrounding the establishment of a customs union. New or unrecognised opportunities are revealed as trade barriers are removed; information and knowledge are neither perfect nor the free commodities they are often assumed to be in economic models. Genuine dynamic gains derive from these changing economic circumstances over time.

It is necessary to differentiate the once-for-all changes resulting from specialisation, economies of scale and competition from the continuing effects resulting from revisions of expectations about the future – and to remember that some revisions somewhere in the union must be downwards! The only attempt so far to assess the indirect effects of a customs union is the NIESR's study of the EEC over a ten-year period [47]. Here the genuine dynamic effects and the once-for-all adjustments are not separated. This study revealed little evidence in the experience of EEC countries to support the claims for substantial economic gains from indirect effects of integration. These results are rather surprising and must be partly due to the formidable methodological problems of measuring the effects of integration in the presence of many other changes in the economic circumstances in the EEC.

Theoretical analysis shows that forming a customs union leads to economic gains from improved allocation of resources for a variety of reasons. Very little attempt has been made, however, to ascertain how benefits are distributed among participating countries. If industrial output in some sectors declines while in others it expands, it is quite possible that, on balance, some participating countries will gain while others lose. Moreover, even if all countries benefit economically, some industrial sectors must undergo considerable adjustments. If there is a rapid expansion in output in the customs union throughout the transition period, the adjustment problems can be eased by transfer payments either between member countries or between sectors in the same country. But this still involves important policy questions that have received scant attention in the literature. The problems of assessing the effects of membership of a customs union on an individual country have been highlighted in the discussion of Britain's proposed entry into the EEC (see HMSO [24] and Williamson [68]).

Finally, it is necessary to point out that this survey of customs unions is concerned with what Pinder has called 'negative integration' [52], that is, the elimination of existing barriers to the movement of goods and services. 'Positive integration' is concerned with active harmonisation of economic policies by the member states. It involves, therefore, a political decision to integrate beyond the simple process of regional free trade, and falls outside this survey. (Johnson [27] and Cooper and Massell [12] have made attempts to show the economic costs of political decisions to pursue a policy of integration – see Section 7 below.) The extent to which policy harmonisation is necessary in order to achieve the benefits of free trade within regional trade agreements has been shown to be far less important than was originally thought (see Johnson, Wonnacott and Shibata [32]).

6 Trade Policy and Development

Trade has been described as an engine of growth. In the nineteenth century this appears to have been true, but changed circumstances and the expansion of protectionism in this century have greatly diminished the transmission effects of trade.

Nurkse [48] has explained how economic growth was transmitted from the focal centre of the world economy to outlying areas in the nineteenth century. The demand for food and basic raw materials in the industrial centre outpaced the development of local supplies, and the deficiency was met from supplies produced in outlying areas. Expanding markets provided new opportunities in the outlying areas which were exploited with the aid of capital and labour transferred from the centre to the peripheral regions, which at that time were principally the areas of recent settlement in Canada, South Africa, Argentina and Australia. The path of economic development under this system was not smooth because any recession at the centre tended to have an immediate impact in the peripheral regions, as reduced demand for primary products, deterioration in the terms of trade and decreases in the flow of investment funds. When the world-wide recession occurred in the 1930s it had especially severe effects in the outlying countries.

During the last two decades many former dependencies have achieved independence, but despite the very rapid growth of trade in manufactured goods the general economic atmosphere handed down from the inter-war period has restricted the opportunities of less developed countries to seek economic development through trade. Advanced industrial countries have preserved highly restrictive policies against agricultural imports and many have tightened restrictions against imports of cheap semi-manufactures and manufactures. In addition, fundamental changes have occurred in many markets of interest to less developed countries' exporters. Technical improvements in extractive methods and the achievements of higher crop yields have tended to shift supply curves to the right, while improved manufacturing processes, permitting economies in the use of raw materials, and the introduction of synthetic substitutes, have tended to shift demand curves to the left. The result has been a downward pressure on primary commodity prices. (For a very clear summary of the issues underlying the trade and aid needs of the less developed countries, see Weintraub [66].)

There have always been dissenters from the traditional view of trade as a transmitter of economic growth. With the increasing concern for poorer countries in recent years the arguments of the critics have strengthened. Writers such as Myrdal, Singer and Prebisch have suggested that instead of waiting for the transmission of development through trade, the poor countries could achieve more rapid development if they concentrated on the expansion of output for domestic markets through import substitution and deliberate policies on industrialisation. Meier [44], in an excellent summary of the debate, points out that the classical view was founded on three different theories of trade: the 'vent for surplus' theory, the static comparative costs theory, and a dynamic 'productivity' theory. The 'productivity' theory provides a link between trade and development, because it interprets trade as a dynamic force widening markets, extending the scope for specialisation, increasing opportunities to use machinery and encouraging the introduction of new techniques.

Myrdal and Singer, on the other hand, have argued that the free play of international forces tends cumulatively to accentuate international economic inequalities. There are three strands to their argument. First, it is alleged that development has been retarded by the unfavourable effects of international factor movements, especially the flow of investment into large-scale commercial plantations, mines, oilfields, etc., which create a 'dual economy' and put undue pressure on the backward rural sector to provide labour employment opportunities. Second, it is claimed that the international operation of the 'demonstration effect' tends to raise the propensity to consume and to limit capital accumulation, which is essential for development. Third, an apparent secular deterioration in the commodity terms of trade is claimed to have caused an international transfer from the poor to the rich countries. This last argument was given particular emphasis by Singer, but in recent years it has been most forcefully represented by Prebisch. Protectionist policies in developed countries, Prebisch [54] argues, restrict the export opportunities and, therefore, the development opportunities of the less developed countries. Meier [44] summarises some powerful counter-arguments that support the traditional theoretical arguments for trade as a stimulant of economic development, and he suggests that the major interferences to this process have come from domestic obstacles in less developed countries.

IMPORT SUBSTITUTION

Trade policies that have been adopted by many less developed countries reflect the weakening acceptance of the traditional role of trade on development following the theoretical criticisms. Protectionist policies aimed at fostering domestic growth accord with recent theoretical attacks on the traditional views and appear also to accord with the autarkic aspirations of leaders in many newly independent states.

The infant industry argument for protection has been accepted as an exception to free trade since the beginning of the nineteenth century. Temporary protection of an industry is supported on the grounds that the existing comparative cost relationships are irrelevant because foreign suppliers established in the market have advantages which if available to the infant industry would enable it to produce at lower costs. The protection is intended to facilitate the channelling of resources into specific industries and to buy time while a protected industry undergoes a learning process to become competitive. Temporarily consumers are taxed and resources transferred to the protected industry. The only economic justification for this is that the social return will exceed the private return from investment in the new industry.

Over time it has been shown that the application of the infant industry argument is heavily circumscribed by qualifications [30]. In particular, the correct selection of genuine infant industries is uncertain in so far as it entails forecasting the potential cost structure of an industry, and its established competitors. Johnson [28] views the infant industry arguments as explicitly dynamic, 'an argument for temporary intervention to correct a transient distortion'. He distinguishes the process of learning-by-doing from the 'external economies' argument; the latter, if they exist, can most efficiently be achieved by means of a combination of domestic taxes and subsidies (see above, pp. 27–9).

In view of the qualifications to the infant industry argument, its extension to support infant economy protection is surrounded with doubt. Myint [46] has pointed out that the essence of the classical infant industry case is its selectivity. Policies of import substitution seek growth through the diversification of production to supply protected domestic markets, while the infant industry argument depends on increased specialisation in the use of resources. The former results in inefficiencies in production, often using expensive capital imports financed from overseas aid programmes, and the consumption of lower-quality, high-cost substitutes. Myint also suggests that concentration on policies of import substitution has, in practice, diverted attention away from opportunities for expanding output and exports of agricultural products; historically, the 'vent for surplus' theory of international trade has played a significant role in economic development.

Johnson [28] and Bhagwati [9] have shown that tariffs are generally a second-best solution to problems of resource allocation associated with domestic distortions. One exception is the infant industry case, which has been shown to be subject to strict qualifications, and the other is the optimum tariff. Evidence for the declining terms of trade of primary producers, which is open to dispute [30], suggests that there is a case for applying the optimum tariff as a means of shifting the

67

distribution of international income in their favour. Less developed countries facing particularly low elasticities of demand for their exports could improve their terms of trade by levying such a tariff, provided the suitable tariff level can be calculated.

EXPORT EXPANSION

Policies of import substitution had brought many less developed countries severe balance of payments difficulties. Consumer-goods industries established behind protective walls involve imports of expensive machinery and intermediate goods, which in the short run may involve a country in greater foreign exchange costs than would be necessary to meet domestic demand for the final products by imports. (The use of scarce foreign exchange and overseas aid for this purpose may be inefficient in terms of development of the economy, although these costs may be partly alleviated if foreign private investment is attracted into the protected market.) Many of these artificially cultivated industries are inefficient and their products costly so that few exports occur. In recent years several countries, such as Brazil, India, Pakistan and Argentina, have recognised the need to develop industries capable of exporting. This shows recognition of the case for traditional free trade, whereby world market forces help to transform their internal economic structure according to potential comparative advantage.

In order to be successful, policies of export expansion depend on improved opportunities to export to developed country markets, as well as policy adjustments in less developed countries. Exports of primary products account for more than 85 per cent of foreign exchange earnings by less developed countries. Hence, as a group they must continue to rely on exports of primary products, which in any case generally offer scope for most rapid expansion of output. Yet the developed countries employ a wide range of trade barriers to restrict these imports, including tariffs, quotas, excise taxes and specific legislative regulations. Johnson [30] examines the impact of particular trade restrictions by dividing primary product exports from less developed countries into three groups:

(i) products that compete with produce from developed countries (metals and some temperate agricultural produce);

(ii) products that do not compete with produce from developed countries (tropical agricultural produce);

(iii) products that compete as substitutes for products from developed countries.

Groups (i) and (iii) provide the most difficulties. Clearly, it will prove difficult to persuade the developed countries to remove or even reduce their agricultural protection, and discussions of international commodity agreements and price-stabilising measures are involved with entrenched positions and prejudices.

Restrictions in developed countries against imports of semi-manufactures and low-cost manufactures have been increasing. Balassa [2] and others have shown how escalation of the tariff structure provides excessive protection for certain industrial activities in developed countries; for example, textiles and certain early stages of processing primary products. On the whole, tariff reductions in GATT have not reduced nominal tariff rates on these items and, in consequence, effective rates of protection have become differentially greater. If policies of export expansion in less developed countries are to be successful, therefore, it is essential that greater opportunities should be provided for them to export this industrial production.

One proposal made at the first UNCTAD was that developed countries should grant temporary tariff preferences for industrial exports from less developed countries. This has been described as a logical extension of the infant industry argument [29]. Instead of transitional support for the industry being given at the expense of domestic consumers, however, the transfer of resources is made from the income of producers and governments in developed countries; both represent a social investment with the return accruing to producers in the infant industries. Under the tariff preference scheme, however, the industries selected for development depend on the tariff structures in the preference-giving countries. This has the effect

69

of encouraging less developed countries to develop the industries that are most protected in developed countries, which need not be related to the pattern of actual or potential comparative costs in the developing countries.

After many years of negotiations an agreement was reached in UNCTAD in October 1970 for the provision of generalised, non-discriminatory, non-reciprocal temporary preferences for industrial exports of developing countries in the markets of developed countries. The initial agreement is for ten years. Some detailed points on reverse preferences and safeguards remain to be resolved, but several major developed countries implemented a variety of discriminatory preference schemes in 1971. It remains to be seen how effectively manufacturing industry in the less developed countries can exploit these opportunities.

REGIONAL TRADE GROUPINGS

Another proposal is a new substitution policy within regional trade groupings of less developed countries. Such preferential trading areas could discriminate in favour of industrial exports from partner countries, and discriminate against exports from developed countries. A logical extension of policies of import substitution, these groupings, by extending the size of the home market, allow scope for economies of scale and specialisation on the basis of comparative advantage.

Customs unions or free trade areas established between less developed countries cannot be assessed in terms of static analysis because the main aim is to facilitate economic growth. An OECD report [34] has indicated the importance of agreed regional investment policy to be implemented and endorsed by all member governments, and/or the need for schemes to compensate member countries left with less than a fair share of the overall benefits. Kojima [35] has developed a theory of 'agreed specialisation' within regional trade groupings, showing how a rational direction of investment resources can avoid duplication of production plant. Although this approach appears to be *dirigiste*, Kojima suggests several ways in which such objectives can be achieved within a system of private enterprise through operations of multinational firms. In Latin America – in LAFTA and the Central American Common Market – complementarity agreements have achieved several successes [61, 62], and the OECD report [34] includes an assessment of existing schemes of integration among less developed countries. The authors conclude that even the most advanced integration schemes in the developing world are still far from reaching their objectives. Policies of agreed specialisation, investment co-ordination and the setting up of institutional machinery involve a considerable sacrifice of political sovereignty.

TRADE OR AID?

The plea 'trade not aid' became a catch-phrase in the 1960s. Since fostering economic development in less developed countries depends upon a transfer of resources from the advanced countries to the less developed countries, there is little sense in making general comparisons between alternative ways of achieving the transfer without referring to the details (see Johnson [30]).

Trade policy can be employed by developing countries to accelerate their economic development, provided the policies operated by other countries, especially developed countries, do not obstruct this objective. Equally, financial aid is often closely linked with trade policy. 'Tied' aid represents an aspect of trade policy by developed countries. 'Untying' aid might allow less developed country recipients to use a given volume of aid more effectively, but from the viewpoint of producers and exporters in donor countries this might represent an unacceptable loss. Similarly, protectionist policies in less developed countries can be employed to attract foreign private investment in specialised manufacturing activities that would not occur without such policies. Finally, official aid flows play a vital role in creating economic infrastructures which contribute to general economic development, including export activities.

7 Concluding Remarks

The theory of international trade has moved closer, in recent years, to providing an explanation of the observed patterns in international trading relations as analysis of trade policy has been incorporated into general equilibrium models. Several theorists have sought to explain trade patterns by attempting to elaborate the basic Heckscher–Ohlin model to give more emphasis to demand forces. These efforts have been expertly synthesised by Johnson [31]. In fashioning a dynamic interpretation of comparative advantage, he has recognised the long-run significance of trade barriers for international patterns of trade and specialisation. Accepting that national differences in factor endowments are one source of comparative advantage, it is still necessary to discover why countries with broadly similar factor ratios can specialise and compete more successfully in different production activities. One source of differences is discontinuities at national frontiers which allow social and cultural differences. These are augmented by differences in government policies, which influence the qualities of factor inputs, through education and research programmes, as well as demand. More particularly, trade policies are used by governments to intensify the boundaries between national markets and obstruct the movements of goods (factor inputs are considered to be internationally immobile in this model). Protection provided by trade interventions induces resources to enter the most protected industrial activities where they can earn higher returns, and this represents one way in which specialisation can evolve. The separation of national markets gives rise to differences in market size too, which enables differences in comparative advantages to arise from differential opportunities to exploit economies of scale in production, marketing and/or technology in particular goods or in particular industries.

In the context of a dynamic world economy, also, trade barriers play a significant role. Economic advantages established behind a protective trade policy can be profitably exploited in other markets if obstructions to the mobility of factors of production can be overcome. The rapid expansion in the activities of multinational corporations derives from a recognition that some factors of production, namely management, technology and investment funds, are readily transferable across many national frontiers; political and economic stability and the revolution in transport and communications in the last twenty years have facilitated this development. One consequence of the increased international mobility of some factor inputs, as demonstrated by the activities of multinational corporations, is that it casts doubt on some aspects of national trade policies, which have evolved from traditional assumptions of international trade theory.

Traditionally, the theory of international trade has treated trade policy as exogenous for purposes of analysis. The rudimentary theory of dynamic comparative advantage indicates that, in practice, trade interventions are an integral part of theory. Another shortcoming of theory, however, is that little consideration has been given to the determination of trade policy, as distinct from analysis of the consequences and desirability of protection. The latter has established that a tariff, for example, is a second-best solution in most economic situations. Yet governments continue to use tariffs as an element in their policies, which suggests that the costs associated with this second-best alternative are somehow acceptable in the context of governments' objectives. Striking examples of 'irrationality' in terms of conventional theory are reciprocal tariff bargaining, the creation of customs unions and the use of protectionist policies to foster economic development.[1] Traditional theory identifies a reduction in tariffs as the source

[1] Cooper and Massell [11, 12], in an exploration of the contribution that customs unions can make to foster economic development, refer to a theoretical dilemma: '. . . the very grounds on which a CU is said to be superior to non-discriminatory protection are precisely those grounds on which the union is necessarily inferior to free trade'.

of gain by replacing domestic output by lower-cost imports. Hence, tariff-distorted trade implies an economic cost in terms of private consumption of goods and services, the orthodox welfare criterion.

Johnson [27] has sketched a theory which incorporates non-economic objectives into the determination of trade policy and which embraces observed trade policies. His hypothesis is that a government's choice represents a rational outcome from offsetting divergences between private and social costs or benefits. Suppose it is decided to seek 'industrialisation'; that is, there exists a collective preference for industrial production for one reason or another. Resources to support this policy, which represents a collective consumption good, can be obtained by various types of government action, including trade policy measures. Rational behaviour by the Government requires that industrial protection (for example, a tariff) should be pursued to the point where the value of collective utility derived from collective consumption of domestic industrial activity is equal to the marginal excess private costs of protected industries. The latter is composed of the marginal private consumption cost (loss of consumers' surplus from the tariff) and the marginal production cost (the proportion by which domestic costs exceed world market costs – the effective protective rate). In this manner, a nation's 'real income', including collective consumption, is maximised, but at the cost of a reduction in 'real product' defined as total production of private goods and services (the orthodox welfare measure). Bhagwati [9] has surveyed the relevance of this theory of trade policy determination to the selection of development policies for less developed countries.

These new approaches to the theory of international trade policy require considerable elaboration and empirical testing before they become generally acceptable. Yet they point the direction in which the theory of trade policy must evolve if it is to contribute, as it must, to the resolution of outstanding international problems of commercial policy.

Select Bibliography

[1] F. A. M. Alting von Geusau (ed.), *Economic Relations after the Kennedy Round* (John F. Kennedy Institute, Centre for Atlantic Studies, Tilburg, Netherlands, 1969).

[2] B. Balassa, 'Tariff Protection in Industrial Countries: An Evaluation', *Journal of Political Economy*, LXXIII (Dec 1965).

[3] B. Balassa, 'Trade Creation and Trade Diversion in the European Common Market', *Economic Journal*, LXXVII (Mar 1967).

[4] R. E. Baldwin, *Non-tariff Distortions of International Trade* (Allen & Unwin, London, 1970).

[5] R. E. Baldwin, 'The Effects of Tariffs on International and Domestic Prices', *Quarterly Journal of Economics*, LXXIV (Feb 1960).

[6] T. S. Barker and S. S. Han, 'Effective Rates of Protection for United Kingdom Production', *Economic Journal*, LXXXI (June 1971).

[7] J. Bhagwati and V. K. Ramaswami, 'Domestic Distortions, Tariffs and the Theory of Optimum Subsidy', *Journal of Political Economy*, LXXI (Feb 1963).

[8] J. Bhagwati, 'On the Equivalence of Tariffs and Quotas', in R. E. Baldwin *et al.*, *Trade, Growth and the Balance of Payments: Essays in Honour of G. Haberler* (North-Holland, Amsterdam, 1966).

[9] J. Bhagwati, *The Theory and Practice of Commercial Policy: Departures from Unified Exchange Rates* (International Finance Section, Princeton University, 1968).

[10] M. Camps, *Britain and the European Community 1955–63* (Oxford U.P., 1964).

[11] C. A. Cooper and B. F. Massell, 'Towards a General Theory of Customs Unions for Developing Countries', *Journal of Political Economy*, LXXIII (Oct 1965).

[12] C. A. Cooper and B. F. Massell, 'A New Look at Customs Union Theory', *Economic Journal*, LXXV (Dec 1965).

[13] J. O. Coppock, *Atlantic Agricultural Unity* (McGraw-Hill, New York, 1966).

[14] H. Corbet and D. Robertson (eds), *Europe's Free Trade Area Experiment* (Pergamon, Oxford, 1970).

[15] W. M. Corden, 'The Structure of a Tariff System and the Effective Protective Rate', *Journal of Political Economy*, LXXIV (June 1966).

[16] W. M. Corden, *The Theory of Protection* (Clarendon Press, Oxford, 1971).

[17] G. Curzon, *Multilateral Commercial Diplomacy* (Michael Joseph, London, 1965).

[18] G. and V. Curzon, *Hidden Barriers to International Trade* (Trade Policy Research Centre, London, 1971).

[19] EFTA Secretariat, *The Effects of EFTA on the Economies of Member States* (EFTA, Geneva, 1969).

[20] B. Fernon, *Issues in World Farm Trade* (Trade Policy Research Centre, London, 1970).

[21] GATT, 'Note on Trends in Sources of European Imports since the Creation of EEC and EFTA', in *International Trade 1966* (GATT Report, Geneva, 1966).

[22] H. G. Grubel and H. G. Johnson, 'Nominal Tariffs, Indirect Taxes and Effective Rates of Protection: The Common Market Countries 1959', *Economic Journal*, LXXVII (Dec 1967). See also [69] below.

[23] G. Haberler, *The Theory of International Trade* (Hodge, London, 1936).

[24] HMSO, *Britain and the European Communities: An Economic Assessment*, Cmnd 4289 (HMSO, London, 1970).

[25] H. G. Johnson, *Money, Trade and Economic Growth* (Allen & Unwin, London, 1962) chap. 3, 'The Economic Theory of Customs Unions'.

[26] H. G. Johnson, *International Trade and Economic Growth* (Allen & Unwin, London, 1958) chap. 2, 'Optimum Tariffs and Retaliation'.

[27] H. G. Johnson, 'An Economic Theory of Protectionism, Tariff Bargaining, and the Formation of Customs Unions', *Journal of Political Economy*, LXXIII (June 1965).

[28] H. G. Johnson, 'Optimal Trade Interventions in the Presence of Domestic Distortions', in R. E. Baldwin *et al.*, *Trade, Growth and the Balance of Payments: Essays in Honour of G. Haberler* (North-Holland, Amsterdam, 1966).

[29] H. G. Johnson, *Aspects of the Theory of Tariffs* (Allen & Unwin, London, 1971).

[30] H. G. Johnson, *Economic Policies towards Less Developed Countries* (Allen & Unwin, London, 1967).

[31] H. G. Johnson, *Comparative Cost and Commercial Policy Theory for a Developing World Economy*, 1968 Wicksell Lectures (Almqvist & Wiksell, Stockholm, 1968).

[32] H. G. Johnson, P. Wonnacott and H. Shibata, *Harmonisation of National Economic Policies under Free Trade*, Canada in the Atlantic Economy, No. 3 (Univ. of Toronto Press, 1968).

[33] T. E. Josling, *Agriculture and Britain's Trade Policy Dilemma* (Trade Policy Research Centre, London, 1971).

[34] F. Kahnert, P. Richards, E. Stoutjesdijk and P. Thomopoulos, *Economic Integration among Developing Countries* (OECD Development Centre, Paris, 1969).

[35] K. Kojima, 'Towards a Theory of Agreed Specialisation: The Economics of Integration', in W. A. Eltis, M. Fg. Scott and J. N. Wolfe (eds), *Induction, Growth and Trade* (Oxford U.P., 1970).

[36] W. W. Leontief, 'The Use of Indifference Curves in the Analysis of Foreign Trade', in A.E.A., *Readings in International Trade* (Allen & Unwin, London, 1950).

[37] R. G. Lipsey and K. J. Lancaster, 'The General Theory of Second Best', *Review of Economic Studies*, xxiv (1956–7).

[38] R. G. Lipsey, 'The Theory of Customs Union: A General Survey', *Economic Journal*, lxx (Sep 1960).

[39] N. Lundgren, 'Customs Unions of Industrialised West European Countries', in G. R. Denton (ed.), *Economic Integration in Europe* (Weidenfeld & Nicolson, London, 1969).

[40] J. Marsh and C. Ritson, *Agricultural Policy and the Common Market* (Chatham House/PEP, London, 1971).

[41] J. E. Meade, *The Theory of International Economic Policy*, vol. ii: *Trade and Welfare* (Oxford U.P., 1955).

[42] J. E. Meade, *A Geometry of International Trade* (Allen & Unwin, London, 1952).

[43] J. E. Meade, *The Theory of Customs Unions* (North-Holland, Amsterdam, 1955).

[44] G. M. Meier, *International Trade and Development* (Harper & Row, New York, 1963).

[45] M. Michaely, 'On Customs Unions and the Gain from Trade', *Economic Journal*, LXXV (Sep 1965).

[46] H. Myint, 'International Trade and the Developing Countries', in P. A. Samuelson (ed.), *International Economic Relations*, Proceedings of the Third Congress of the International Economic Association, Montreal (Macmillan, London, 1969).

[47] National Institute of Economic and Social Research, 'Another Look at the Common Market', *National Institute Review* (Nov 1970).

[48] R. Nurkse, *Patterns of Trade and Development*, 1959 Wicksell Lectures (Blackwell, Oxford, 1962).

[49] G. Ohlin, 'Trade in a *non-laissez-faire* World', in P. A. Samuelson (ed.), *International Economic Relations*, Proceedings of the Third Congress of the International Economic Association, Montreal (Macmillan, London, 1969).

[50] G. Patterson, *Discrimination in International Trade: The Policy Issues 1945–65* (Princeton U.P., 1966).

[51] I. F. Pearce, *International Trade*, 2 vols (Macmillan, London, 1970).

[52] J. Pinder, 'Problems of European Integration', in G. R. Denton (ed.), *Economic Integration in Europe* (Weidenfeld & Nicolson, London, 1969).

[53] Political and Economic Planning, *European Unity: Co-operation and Integration* (Allen & Unwin, London, 1968).

[54] R. Prebisch, *Towards a New Trade Policy for Development* (United Nations, New York, 1964).

[55] P. A. Samuelson, 'The Gains from International Trade Once Again', *Economic Journal*, LXXII (Dec 1962).

[56] T. Scitovsky, *Economic Theory and Western European Integration* (Allen & Unwin, London, 1958).

[57] R. Shone, *The Pure Theory of International Trade*, Macmillan Studies in Economics (Macmillan, London, 1972).

[58] W. F. Stolper and P. A. Samuelson, 'Protection and Real Wages', *Review of Economic Studies*, IX (Nov 1941).

[59] D. Swann, *The Economics of the Common Market*, Penguin Modern Economics (Penguin Books, Harmondsworth, 1970).

[60] E. M. Truman, 'The European Economic Community: Trade Creation and Trade Diversion', *Yale Economic Essays* (spring 1969).

[61] United Nations, *Trade in Manufactures of Developing Countries: 1970 Review*.

[62] UNCTAD Secretariat, *Trade Expansion and Economic Integration among Developing Countries* (United Nations, New York, 1967).

[63] J. Vanek, *International Trade: Theory and Economic Policy* (Irwin, Homewood, Ill., 1962) part IV.

[64] J. Vanek, *General Equilibrium of International Discrimination* (Harvard U.P., Cambridge, Mass., 1965).

[65] J. Viner, *The Customs Union Issue* (Carnegie Endowment, New York, 1950).

[66] S. Weintraub, *The Foreign Exchange Gap of Developing Countries* (International Finance Section, Princeton University, 1965).

[67] S. J. Wells, *International Economics* (Allen & Unwin, London, 1969).

[68] J. Williamson, 'Trade and Economic Growth', in J. Pinder (ed.), *The Economics of Europe* (Charles Knight, London, 1971).

[69] H. G. Grubel and H. G. Johnson (eds.), *Effective Tariff Protection* (GATT and Graduate Institute of International Studies, Geneva, 1971).